Orders:
Box 20725
Birmingham, AL 35216

Editorial Address:
3601 Westbury Road
Birmingham, AL 35223

Michel de Saint Pierre

Michel de Saint Pierre

A Catholic Novelist at the Crossroads

by

David O'Connell

SUMMA PUBLICATIONS, INC.
Birmingham, Alabama
1990

For Dan, Andrew, and Jim

Table of Contents

Acknowledgments

This study has been enriched by the support and advice of a number of colleagues. In France, I would like to thank Mahaut Pascalis at Editions de la Table Ronde and Suzanne Lescoat at Editions Calmann-Lévy, who provided invaluable assistance in allowing me access to the press clippings generated by Michel de Saint Pierre's books.

Michel de Saint Pierre himself, during the last seven years of his life, also allowed me access to much information that has been useful in the present work. Since then his widow, Mme Jacqueline de Saint Pierre, has continued to be of great help to me. To her I express my debt of gratitude.

On this side of the Atlantic, Professor Albert Sonnenfeld, through his own writings on the subject of the Catholic novel and his personal support of this book, has been of immeasurable assistance. I am indebted to him for his long and consistent support. I would also like to express my thanks to Professor William Cloonan who read the manuscript and made many helpful suggestions. Of course, any oversights, omissions, or errors of judgment that appear in these pages are mine exclusively.

Finally, I would like to express my deep appreciation to my wife Kathy for her constant support during the years I worked on this project.

—*David O'Connell*

1. A Writer's Vocation

MICHEL DE SAINT PIERRE DIED ON JUNE 19, 1987 AT HIS COUNTRY home in Normandy. Two days earlier, he had completed his last novel, *Le Milieu de l'été*, a work that he had written while convalescing from surgery and prolonged medical treatment for a chronic heart problem. He has left behind him more than forty titles ranging from the novel, on which his reputation is based, to history, biography, theater, and polemic.

For some forty years he had been recognized in France as a Catholic writer, an epithet that is avoided by virtually all Catholics who write since it threatens to limit in the minds of critics both the scope of their work and their possible appeal to readers. Like François Mauriac before him, who preferred to be known as a "Catholic who writes novels" rather than as a "Catholic writer," Saint Pierre accepted the label but was uncomfortable with it, especially in the last fifteen years or so of his life. In fact, starting about 1970, he preferred to be called an "écrivain témoin de son temps," even though *La Passion de l'abbé Delance* (1978) and *Le Milieu de l'été* (1987) are clearly "Catholic novels." Like Balzac, whose careful method of documentation he imitated as he set about writing each of his novels, Saint Pierre sought to enter into dialogue with readers of all backgrounds, not only those who shared his religious background and personal convictions.

Saint Pierre wrote from a somewhat unique perspective. As a traditional Catholic he was against most of the changes brought about by Vatican II, and as an aristocrat he remained a committed monarchist until the day he died. Having worked for a living his whole life, however, he was a social and economic pragmatist, as his novels amply demonstrate. Thus, not only did he not reject outright the idea of progress, which has traditionally been a common reaction among people from his background, he in fact devoted many of his novels (especially those published after 1970) to the changes that were taking place in French society during his lifetime.

The present study seeks to demonstrate that despite the general lack of critical interest displayed in recent years in the Catholic novel in France, there still exist writers in France who work in this genre. Although there continues to be a lively scholarly interest in Catholic writers who established themselves in the interwar years, like Bernanos, Mauriac or Green, and who continued their work after the war for varying lengths of time, there has been a tendency to neglect Catholic writers of later generations, particularly those who belong to what we can call the generation of 1915. This generation, which followed upon the generation of 1900, of which Julien Green is the most prominent writer of fiction, came two generations behind the great generation of 1885, which boasts, in addition to Mauriac and Bernanos, giants like Teilhard de Chardin, Gilson, and Maritain.

In deciding to devote the present study to the novels of Michel de Saint Pierre as a representative of the generation of 1915, I had to choose from among a number of possible candidates, including Patrice de la Tour du Pin (1911-75), Luc Estang (1911-), Jacques de Bourbon Busset (1912-), Gilbert Cesbron (1913-79), Paul-André Lesort (1915-), Pierre Emmanuel (1916-83), Roger Bésus (1915-), Jean Sulivan (1913-80), and Maurice Clavel (1920-79).[1] The reasons that dictated the choice of Saint Pierre as an exemplar of this ongoing phenomenon of the Catholic novelist in France are several in number. First, he has made his mark primarily in one genre, the novel. Like Mauriac and Bernanos, he also did a good deal of work as a journalist, pamphleteer, and biographer, but his main creative efforts were devoted to the novel. This concentration makes it somewhat easier to evaluate his achievement.

Secondly, during his long career, Saint Pierre had the largest readership of any Catholic novelist in France, especially after the death of Gilbert Cesbron in 1980. While, admittedly, quantity does not insure quality, it does not necessarily preclude it either. A natural storyteller, Saint Pierre had the knack over more than three decades of selecting for his novels topics that were able to attract a wide audience. In fact, in the case of what is surely his best as well as his most renowned novel, *Les Nouveaux Prêtres* (1964), the subject of the book (the "new priests" emerging in France as the Second Vatican Council was unfolding) was already a widely debated topic before the novel appeared. Taking a very definite ideological position in that debate, the novel had all the ingredients for popular success and indeed was a tremendous best-seller. Unfortunately, the controversy that the book created caused critics to lose sight of its real merits as a work of literature.

While it is in the nature of best-sellers to be remarkably successful before gradually going out of print, this has not been the case with Saint Pierre's best novels, most of which continue to be republished year after year in paperback edition. Thus, in an era when the definition of what it means to be a Catholic novelist has become more problematical, Saint Pierre has remained the most visible and widely read French Catholic novelist of his generation during the past three decades.

A third reason for selecting Saint Pierre and his work for closer scrutiny is that his experience reflects better than that of any of his contemporaries the dilemma of the Catholic novel and the Catholic novelist over the course of the last forty years. Michel de Saint Pierre's career was punctuated in mid-course by the eruption of the Second Vatican Council. The world of inherited belief and ritual in which the Catholic novelist had traditionally worked evaporated within the space of a few years. As a novelist who was making his reputation as a Catholic writer under the Fourth Republic, Saint Pierre found both the religious and social underpinnings of his life and career swept from under him by the arrival, at only a few years' interval, first of the Council (1961-65) and then of the sociological and technological transformations of the sixties and seventies that had begun with the return to power of General De Gaulle and the foundation of the Fifth Republic in 1958. Saint Pierre's work could not help but be influenced by the Council, and one of the goals of this study will be to show how, as both a writer and a believer, he had to adapt his material—as well as his treatment of that material—to new and evolving realities.

Although there has been a sharp decline in religious practice in France in the past twenty years, the overwhelming changes that have taken place in a society that was the least advanced technologically in Western Europe when De Gaulle came to power have made many Frenchmen nostalgic for their roots and for traditional, stable values. Ironically, while Saint Pierre the public figure defended traditional values and lamented the existence of the present Socialist regime in France, his novels clearly welcomed the new society and accepted many of the changes that have taken place while at the same time pointing out that scientific and technical advances do not alter the basics of human nature.

A fourth reason for studying Saint Pierre's *œuvre* is to point out relationships and discordances between Saint Pierre's fiction and that of novelists of an earlier generation, particularly Mauriac and Bernanos. Saint Pierre's world view is decidedly less gloomy than that of his two predecessors. In addition, his technique, his way of presenting character and incident, was always less interested in deep psychological analysis than in showing how people act and talk. There is thus what we can call a certain "cinematic" quality to Saint Pierre's fiction that obliges the reader to make judgments about characters based on what they say and do rather than on what an omniscient narrator tells us about them.

A fifth reason for examining closely Saint Pierre's career is that he offers an interesting case history of what lies in store for a writer whose work goes against the prevailing intellectual currents of his age. Every student of French literature is aware of the importance of trends and fads in French intellectual life. In the last half century, the socially conscious novel of the thirties has given way successively in the postwar era to existentialism, the *nouveau roman,* structuralism, post-structuralism, and semiology, among others. The proliferation of the adjective "nouveau" highlights this tendency, for in the past thirty years we have seen, in addition to the *nouveau roman,* the *nouvelle vague* in cinema, the *nouvelle cuisine* in gastronomy, the *nouveau théâtre* in drama production, and *les nouveaux philosophes* in the political and philosophical essay. The *nouveau roman,* with its emphasis on *chosisme,* characterized by the minute description of physical detail, and its strident attacks on the traditional novel that tells a story in a conventional manner, did succeed for a period of time in inflicting what the French call "terrorisme intellectuel" on young, aspiring novelists.[2] This fear of doing something that might be out of step with the prevailing Latin Quarter credo among reigning intellectuals—like writing a novel that tells a story, that has characters who live in a world that the average person can recognize, and that has a beginning, a middle, and an end—has probably been one of the main contributing factors to the decline in prestige of French literature since the sixties. As John Ardagh says of the practitioners of the *nouveau roman:* "Their influence seems to have been mainly negative. For some years Robbe-Grillet and others exerted a kind of tyranny over younger novelists, making them feel unable to write in a traditional manner any more; and only now is the novel beginning to recover from this and return to humanistic values."[3] He goes on to point out that with "the waning of the experimental novel, the literary trend now is back to books that tell stories and develop characters. Yet it is remarkable how few of these deal squarely with themes of contemporary France."[4]

Michel de Saint Pierre, whose novels have dealt over the past forty years with a wide array of contemporary social problems, stands out as someone who has been unafraid to disregard prevailing fads and to give us a series of novels, in the tradition of Balzac, that are based on minute observation of characters presented against the background of a rapidly changing society. Once again, to quote Ardagh, "It seems a pity, when French society has been going through so fascinating a period of transition, that the novel has virtually abdicated its classic Balzacian role as chronicler of that society."[5] It is my conviction that Saint Pierre's widespread popularity and vast reading public are due in large part to the fact that his novels take as their primary subject matter the tensions and dilemmas of modern French life.

When Pope John XXIII announced in 1960 his intention to convoke a Second Vatican Council[6] in order to update the Catholic Church and attempt to lessen its sense of isolation from the modern world, Michel de Saint Pierre was in his mid-forties and had been publishing novels since 1948. Born into an aristocratic Norman family, Saint Pierre was the son of a retired army officer who was wounded four times and cited for valor on several occasions during World War I. A career military officer, the "marquis" as he was called, took his retirement in the twenties, withdrew to the family estate in Normandy, and there set about researching and writing a series of historical studies including biographies of Rollo, the first Duke of Normandy, and, in the Napoleonic era, of Marshall Soult, one of his wife's ancestors, and was working on a history of the Vikings when he died in 1964.[7] Michel de Saint Pierre, like his father, whom he always considered to have been his best friend, displayed over the years a deep respect and reverence for his roots, the places that he and his family come from, and the moral and chivalrous values, those rich intangibles, that make him, and them, what they are. In fact, one personality trait that he may very well have inherited from his father was his outspoken fearlessness in pursuing a course of action against all odds, even to the point of seeming ridiculously quixotic, whenever he perceived it to be his duty to do so. As proof of this penchant, one need only cite his avowed sympathy for monarchy and the monarchist cause in France, despite the fact that is clearly doubtful to most observers that France will ever give herself a king again. His support in the early sixties for the cause of *Algérie française,* followed by his later pleas for amnesty for those Frenchmen who had been arrested for breaking the law in their attempts to keep Algeria as a part of France, also indicate his courage to express what is clearly a minority viewpoint.[8] During the late sixties and all through the seventies, he was outspoken in his support of Mgr. Lefebvre and other Catholic "intégristes" in the face of the growing liberalism (what he called "progressisme") of the French clergy as well as of the majority of active Catholics. In the early eighties, he was in the fore-front, from the very beginning of the Socialist regime, of those French Catholics who voiced their concern about the Socialist plan to nationalize France's Catholic schools. As it turned out, a broad consensus developed around this issue among Frenchmen of widely varying personal, religious, and political points of view, so that in the end the proposal was shelved and the Prime Minister whose name had been associated with it, Pierre Mauroy, stepped down in 1984. Significantly, however, Saint Pierre had been one of the first to man the barricades on this issue, and it turned out to be the only occasion in which the point of view that he supported seems to have triumphed in the public arena.[9]

Saint Pierre's intellectual life entered a rapid cycle of development with his enrollment, at the age of fourteen, in Saint-Jean-de-Béthune, a Catholic secondary school in Versailles. The school was directed by the Eudist fathers, an order founded in Caen in the seventeenth century, and the years spent there played an important role in his overall intellectual and spiritual development, even though, in terms of class standing, he was not a brilliant student. But the intensely lived atmosphere of faith built around daily attendance at mass, the enchantment of the yearly cycle of class and holidays intimately bound up with the beauty and mystery of the liturgical year, the long hours devoted to sports as well as to study, and the camara-derie enjoyed with fellow students, all had a lasting and positive effect on him. These years reaffirmed his faith and seem to have gradually revealed to him two major conclusions about himself: that as an adult he wanted to maintain his independence, and that the best way for him to learn about life and the world would be primarily through experience and only secondarily through books and formal learning. If we judge by the number of his novels in which adolescents are portrayed, from *Ce Monde ancien* (1948) to *Le Double Crime de l'impasse Salomon* (1984), we can begin to appreciate the importance that he attached to this period in his own life.[10]

Not an exemplary student, Saint Pierre was barely able to pass the *baccalauréat* examination at the conclusion of his secondary studies. But with this diploma in hand, he went ahead and, as expected of him in his family and social milieu, enrolled at the Sorbonne at age eighteen and stayed for one year. Sitting in Sorbonne lecture halls while hearing the sounds of the world go by outside proved to be too much for him. The lectures seemed moribund and the life of a student seemed pointless and parasitical. At the end of the year he passed his exams and in so doing proved to himself and his family that he was capable of organized intellectual labor. But that was enough. He withdrew from the university and took a job in September 1935 in the shipyards of Saint-Nazaire in Brittany.

The year that Saint Pierre spent from 1935 to 1936 as a manual worker in the shipbuilding industry is also one of the most important ones for the French working class in this century. For until the victory at the polls of Léon Blum's Popular Front government coalition of Communists, Socialists, and Radicals, French workers still received low wages and no guaranteed paid vacation. He spent the year leading up to this Popular Front victory as a worker who shared the frustration and humiliation of his fellow laborers. He also supported their goals at the same time as he disapproved of many of their methods. For instance, to Saint Pierre the labor strategy based on the general strike did not sufficiently take into account the thousands of workers who either did not believe in, or could not afford to support, such radical measures. As a Catholic, he was also angered by the pomp and ceremony organized by the Left in imitation of Catholic ritual. The massive rallies and the singing of the *Internationale* were one thing, but the perverted theology of Marxism with its prophets (Marx and Engels), its chosen people (the working class) and clergy (party members), its equivalent of Satan (the bourgeois ruling class), its saints and martyrs, and its promise of salvation—a materialistic paradise on earth—were things that he could not accept. In the summer of 1936, the victory of the Popular Front was no great cause for joy for the anti-Communist in Saint Pierre, but he was nonetheless happy to see the living conditions of the average worker improved. At this point, however, further adventure beckoned, and he left the shipyards to join the Navy. Later, when the war was over and the time had come to begin seriously his career as a writer, these experiences as a student in Paris and as a manual worker would become the basis of his first novel, *Ce Monde ancien* (1948).

Beginning his four years of naval service in September 1936, Saint Pierre could of course have no way of knowing that he would not return to a normal civilian way of life until 1945 and the end of World War II. The four years of naval duty, with their strict discipline, would later be transposed in his second novel, *La Mer à boire* (1951). After the defeat of France, Saint Pierre went directly from the Navy into the Resistance movement where he led a very secretive life about which we have been able to reconstruct relatively little. It is a fact that after the war he received several medals and citations for his Resistance efforts, but on the whole he has not written much about this period of his life. Except for one brief section in *Je reviendrai sur les ailes de l'aigle* (1975), in which he transposes this experience through the characters Michel Cohen and Bruno Martinville, there are no other insights into this period of his life to be found in the novels.

From the publication of *Ce Monde ancien* until his death, Saint Pierre's personal biography and his career as a writer largely overlapped. Most of his daily energies were devoted to his work. While the scope of the present study will concentrate on his fictional *œuvre,* in which he begins by seeing himself primarily as a "romancier catholique" or as an "écrivain chrétien," and only later becomes more conscious of his vocation as an "écrivain témoin de son temps," it would be a mistake to ignore the existence of approximately twenty volumes of biography, polemic, and travel literature that he wrote during this same period. As might be expected, the same major themes to be found in his novels are also reflected in these other works, but a detailed analysis of their content would cause us to stray too far from our chief concern, the novels. It can be said, however, that his rejection of what he calls modernism, which implies the celebration of the rights of the individual at the expense of the group, as well as the triumph of the notion of relativism in what had formerly been doctrinal matters, returns in virtually all these works. Examples of strong polemical works in which he finds modernism to be extant and flourishing within the very fabric of the church are *Sainte Colère* (1965), *Eglises en ruines, Eglise en péril* (1973), *Les Fumées de Satan* (1976), and *Le Ver est dans le fruit* (1978).

Likewise, a second theme, the desire for purity and a respect, even a nostalgia, for traditional Catholic teachings in this area, are reflected in his biographies of Saint Bernadette (*Bernadette et Lourdes,* 1952) and the Curé of Ars (*La Vie prodigieuse du curé d'Ars,* 1959). This theme is often presented through Saint Pierre's avowal of his special reverence for priests whom he saw as being specially marked by Christ. Unfortunately, the genuinely saintly priest is sometimes unappreciated, even persecuted by his ecclesiastical superiors. In addition to the biographies just mentioned, this theme also recurs in polemical works like *Sainte Colère* (1965) and *Ces prêtres qui souffrent* (1966), as well as in two major fictional efforts *Les Nouveaux Prêtres* (1964) and *La Passion de l'abbé Delance* (1978). A third major theme is his generous and warm-hearted sympathy for adolescents (as well as for those adults who do not succeed well in France's educational system and who are therefore often relegated to working class status for the rest of their lives). In addition to polemical works like *La Nouvelle Race* (1961), *L'Ecole de la violence* (1962), and *La Jeunesse et l'amour* (1969), we also find this theme in novels like *Les Nouveaux Aristocrates* (1960) and *Laurent* (1980). Finally, Saint Pierre is remarkable as a French novelist in the French Catholic tradition who also has a well-balanced and healthy respect for the body and its functions. One cannot help but be struck by the recurrence in his novels of the legitimate rejoicing in a good meal highlighted by fine wines as a fitting recompense for a day of work. Sexual pleasure is also portrayed as a legitimate display of love between spouses. The guilt associated with sex, the idea that sexual intercourse between spouses is a "souillure," a term used so often by Mauriac's omniscient narrator, is strikingly and refreshingly absent from Saint Pierre's writings, especially his novels.

Defining what we mean when we talk about a Catholic writer or a Catholic novel can be a confusing enterprise. J. C. Whitehouse makes a useful distinction between two kinds of Catholic writing. The first is described as "practical and calculating" and "is aimed ultimately at influence and control."[11] As an example of this type of Catholic writing, he cites "all kinds of theology from St. John the Evangelist to Rosemary Haughton or Teilhard de Chardin, liturgical and devotional works, apologetics and polemics." Of course, many modern Catholic writers, including Saint Pierre himself, have done this kind of writing. Whitehead characterizes the second type of writing as "meditative and reflective, receptive rather than dominating." The writer of the second category works in the realm of the imaginary and has "a sensibility formed and influenced by a specific faith, which contains concepts of man's nature and destiny." Thus, his work is an "expression of a personal reaction to human life and a personal vision of it." Often, the second type of Catholic writer can produce work that has more in common with that of an agnostic or atheistic writer, than with the nonliterary and demonstrative writing of the first category. John

Cruickshank adds another important element to the definition when he writes that as a believer, the Catholic novelist "regards no portrayal of human experience as complete unless it takes into account an element of divine transcendance operative in human affairs. He is thus faced with the formally paradoxical task of translating the ineffable into words, of setting forth convincing human evidence of divine providence."[12] What this means in practical terms is that the truly Catholic novel has the ability to function on two levels, that is, to imply strongly the active operation of invisible powers while remaining comprehensible and credible to eyes that do not acknowledge such powers.[13]

Practitioners of the Catholic novel—François Mauriac and Graham Greene are probably quoted the most often in this regard—have often been cited as saying that there is no such thing as a Catholic novelist, merely Catholics who write novels. We are inclined to agree with this statement, provided that it be understood that the Catholic novelist, because of his beliefs, will often unconsciously inject them into his work and that there is no general rule or formula that can be applied either to a novelist or his work to measure its specific catholicity. As Maurice Bruézière puts it:

> On peut être écrivain de métier et catholique de confession sans être, pour autant, un écrivain catholique. On a réservé cette appellation aux créateurs qui ont intimement mêlé leur foi religieuse à leur inspiration. Pour un Mauriac ou un Bernanos, cette présence de la foi dans l'œuvre n'est pas discutable. Plus discrète chez un Jouhandeau, se confondant parfois, chez Green, avec le sentiment de l'invisible, elle n'est pas moins latente, diffuse chez ces deux auteurs et permet de les inscrire, eux aussi, dans la lignée multiforme de la littérature catholique.[14]

One advantage of Bruézière's yardstick—with which I agree—is its flexibility: there are varying degrees of catholicity in Catholic writers and their work. Bruézière might have added that within a given writer's *œuvre,* some novels are clearly more Catholic than others. For instance, of Mauriac's many novels, *La Pharisienne* (1941) is far more Catholic than any of this other novels. As Jacques Petit points out in his copious and judicious notes to the Pléiade edition of the novel, ". . . *La Pharisienne* est le roman de Mauriac le plus explicitement religieux; un des rares où apparaisse un prêtre qui ne soit pas une esquisse, sinon une caricature; le seul où la vie religieuse des personnages devient une matière romanesque, et même le sujet."[15] While this is true of Mauriac, one would be hard pressed in examining Bernanos's *œuvre* to find a novel that is less overtly Catholic than the others, for they all sound the depths of temptation and sin and strive to present the idea of Evil as an objective reality. In this respect, one can say that Saint Pierre's fictional *œuvre*, when looked at in its totality, is more like that of Mauriac than Bernanos, because some of his novels are decidedly more Catholic in subject matter, as well as in the treatment of that subject matter, than others.

Perhaps it is for this reason that Albert Sonnenfeld prefers to talk about the Catholic novel than about the Catholic novelist or Catholic writer. "There is something called the Catholic Novel: it is a novel written by a Catholic, using Catholicism as its informing mythopoeic structure or generative symbolic system, and where the principal and decisive issue is the salvation or damnation of the hero or heroine."[16] This question of salvation or damnation is a key ingredient in determining the degree to which we can call a work a "Catholic novel." Using it, we can more easily understand that in Saint Pierre's *œuvre*, the truly Catholic novels are really only six in number: *Les Murmures de Satan, Les Ecrivains, Les Nouveaux Aristocrates, Les Nouveaux Prêtres, La passion de l'abbé Delance,* and *Le Milieu de l'été.* While the others all raise in some way issues that are critical to Catholic belief, they do so in a less immediate way. Despite this difference in what we might call Catholic intensity in some of the novels, he does remain overall a Catholic novelist, even in those works that are "less Catholic."

Since Catholic scholars and critics began to chronicle in a serious way the achievements of Catholic novelists in the thirties, there has never been unanimous agreement on who is "Catholic" in his creative work and who is not. For instance, Jean Calvet, in his seminal study, *Le Renouveau catholique dans la littérature contemporaine,* dismissed Bernanos in one sentence. "Les trois romans de Bernanos," he wrote, "sont d'une audace trop nue et d'un mysticisme discutable."[17] For this reason Bernanos was eliminated from serious consideration. As for Mauriac, Calvet did not even consider him to be a Catholic novelist. Categorized with several other minor novelists of the day as a Catholic who does not bring his faith to bear in his fictional writing, Mauriac was simply dismissed. "Ne seraient-ils donc pas catholiques? Ils le sont; mais ils n'ont pas voulu écrire des romans catholiques; pour reprendre une formule de Péguy, ils sont des catholiques écrivains et non des écrivains catholiques. Ils n'appartiennent donc pas à mon sujet."[18] Applying Whitehouse's useful distinction mentioned above, we see that for Calvet Catholic writing, even in fiction, had as its first priority to exercise control and domination over the reader, guiding him to a discovery of church doctrine. If it did not fulfill this essential requirement, it could not be considered as a truly Catholic novel.

A generation later, Jean-Laurent Prévost, who devoted several books to this subject in the fifties, was not yet quite sure whether Saint Pierre could be considered as a Catholic novelist. "Ces problèmes," he wrote, referring to several themes in the novelist's work, "on les retrouve chez un jeune écrivain comme Michel de Saint Pierre; mais si l'on ne savait qu'il dirige des collections apologétiques, et qu'il écrit une *Sainte Berna-dette,* on ne découvrirait pas l'auteur catholique dans ses deux derniers romans, *Les Aristocrates* (1954) et *Les Ecrivains* (1957)."[19] It was admittedly still too early to tell in what direction Saint Pierre was moving, but with the publication of *Les Murmures de Satan, Les Nouveaux Aristocrates,* and *Les Nouveaux Prêtres,* it would become clear that Saint Pierre was a "Catholic novelist" as well as a "Catholic writer." Gérard Mourgue, writing just a few years later, could clearly see that Saint Pierre was emerging as a significant Catholic novelist. Since he had just published *Les Murmures de Satan* and *Les Nouveaux Aristocrates,* his intention to use specifically Catholic material in his novels was becoming more and more apparent. To Mourgue, it was obvious that the God alluded to in Saint Pierre's fiction is "le Dieu des catholiques," and that he was consciously attempting in his work to update and rework the Catholic novel. Wrote Mourgue: "l'effort de rénovation, sur un terrain aussi connu, va donc être d'autant plus difficile."[20] While reserving final judgment on Saint Pierre's accomplishments as a novelist, Mourgue nonetheless confirmed that a new hand was at work in the task of revitalizing the Catholic novel.

The changes that have swept through French society in the past twenty-five years have been far-reaching, and Catholics in France, both as individuals and as members of the church, have been involved in this process as much as anyone else. In fact, Catholics as a group have been more concerned with changes that have taken place in the expressions of their spiritual life than they ever were in all the preceding generations, at least as far back as the Reformation. As Bernard Gouley puts it in the introduction to his enormously important study of the contemporary church in France, *Les Catholiques français d'aujourd'hui: survol d'un peuple,*

> Les superlatifs manquent aux commentateurs pour qualifier la crise qui a
> secoué le catholicisme français depuis un quart de siècle. Rien de com-
> parable depuis Dioclétien, dit l'un. Secousse tellurique, renchérit
> l'autre. Il est vrai que du tremblement de terre cette crise a eu
> l'ampleur, et aussi, à l'échelle du siècle, la soudaineté. . . car les ondes
> de choc ont ébranlé une Eglise solide, sûre d'elle-même, qui croyait
> avoir surmonté les difficultés de son époque.[21]

In opposition to the interwar years, which René Rémond has often called
the "âge d'or du catholicisme français,"[22] and which were in retrospect a
relatively static era which saw the flowering of the works of writers like
Bernanos and Mauriac, the last quarter century has been characterized by so
much change and tension that the idea of the Catholic novelist and his vocation has at times been lost from view. The number of books and articles
devoted to the subject has contracted quite sharply since the mid-sixties.
French Catholic intellectuals, more concerned about interaction with the
world, have lost interest in what at first sight might seem like a dreadfully
parochial concern: the Catholic novel. In one of the most significant
studies to be devoted to the topic in recent years, Joseph Majault has
attempted to describe the main areas of concern of Catholic writers, many of
whom have stopped writing fiction in favor of the essay and the diary,
which are seen as being more sincere and less contrived. Majault writes:

> Car l'espérance du peuple de Dieu ne se porte plus vers les marbres, les
> ors et les indults. Elle resurgit, libre et nue, hors des contraintes des
> siècles passés. Ce n'est plus l'air de la loi qui définit l'amour mais
> c'est de l'amour que procède la loi. Ce n'est plus l'autorité qui impose
> la règle, c'est une allégeance personnelle et réfléchie qui fait adhérer à
> l'organisation. La soumission et la servitude qu'exigeait un code établi
> au fil du temps par une hiérarchie plus désireuse de perpétuer son
> hégémonie que de prêter secours et aide à la communauté, la fidelité
> aveugle qui était requise, ne sont plus aujourd'hui que des vestiges en
> voie de décomposition, d'effritement. On ne plie plus le genou sous le
> joug. La crainte des anathèmes et des excommunications est devenue
> obsolète. Et depuis longtemps déjà les saintes inquisitions ne laissent
> plus en mémoire que les images sanglantes et horribles de
> l'intolérance.[23]

To Majault, the post Vatican II Catholic writer should be primarily interested in the mystery of existence and forsake any notion of certitude. "Entre l'absurde et le mystère," he writes, echoing Jean Guitton, "j'ai choisi le mystère."

Michel de Saint Pierre, who never hid his doubts about many of the changes that have taken place because of Vatican II, did nonetheless share Majault's concern for probing the mystery of existence, which has been one of the primary areas of concern of the Catholic novel over the past century. As a witness to his age as well as an "écrivain catholique," Saint Pierre continued to sort out the good from the bad, to attempt to go along with the changes that were taking place in society while pointing out, when appropriate, things that ought to be retained from earlier generations. It is this tension between the old and the new, the weight of tradition and the call of modernity, that make Saint Pierre's work so interesting and, in my view, worthy of further study and recognition. The present study is a first step in this direction.

2. The Early Fiction

CE MONDE ANCIEN TELLS OF THE COMING OF AGE, BEGINNING IN 1935, of two young men, Gilles de Lointrain, a student of history at the Sorbonne and scion of an upper bourgeois family like that of Saint Pierre himself, and René le Steyr, the son and grandson of manual workers.[1] A reader familiar with the principal facts of Saint Pierre's life cannot escape noticing that the author has divided himself (and parts of his life experience up to that point), between the two young men. Each protagonist's story is recounted separately from January 1935 through the summer of 1936 at which time each of them will make a major decision that will influence him for the rest of his life. René le Steyr will leave his job at the shipyards in Saint-Nazaire to try to make his fortune in Paris. At the same time, Gilles de Lointrain, in full revolt against his bourgeois milieu, will have decided to try to learn more about the world and his place in it by taking a job as a manual laborer in the very shipyards that Le Steyr is leaving. They pass each other in transit and briefly sit side by side at a railway buffet in the last scene of the novel. Although they do not speak to each other, they have been brought together symbolically, for each in a way is an aspect of the fledgling author's personality. Furthermore, although Gilles is aware of René's presence when he overhears him speaking to the owner of the buffet, who has just offered him a job as a waiter, which René refuses, the two characters are nonetheless fundamentally distinct. Saint Pierre's interest in young people, from late adolescence through early adulthood, will recur repeatedly in the later novels, from *Les Aristocrates* and *Les Nouveaux Aristocrates* in the fifties and sixties to *Laurent* in the seventies and *Dr. Erikson* and *Le Double Crime de l'impasse Salomon* in the eighties.

The opening pages of the novel, which reveal what would later become evident as Saint Pierre's lifelong professional debt to Balzac, are also typical of the writer's technique. This novel, like virtually each one that would follow, contains a striking opening scene that attracts the reader's attention and lures him into the story. Here the scene is set in a large lecture hall at the Sorbonne. M. Mothe, a living caricature of a French university professor in the traditional, pre-1968 mold, is giving a lecture on Robert de Sorbon and, in so doing, argues in cumbersome and somewhat boring detail that Sorbon was named chancellor of the institution that bears his name in the year 1257 and not in 1258 as other scholars have claimed. As Mothe continues his lecture, reading slowly and carefully from prepared notes and without looking at his audience, he is oblivious of the fact that many students are paying no attention to him. Gilles de Lointrain in particular is seething with anger and frustration because to him the lecture is meaningless. Determined to display his revolt, yet unsure of what that revolt will gain for him, he raises his hand to ask a question. When M. Mothe recognizes him, he asks: "Je voudrais savoir pourquoi vous abîmez l'histoire" (12). Mothe is shocked and a look of disbelief comes over his face. He then asks Gilles to repeat the question, which he does. By now students are shouting and whistling, "les cris d'animaux jaillirent à nouveau des gradins" (13), and in the uproar Gilles forgets to read all of his prepared speech, but does proclaim the final line of his text: "Je n'étais pas venu ici pour apprendre à empailler l'Histoire de France" (12). Trembling, M. Mothe descends from the lectern, puts on his coat, and leaves the room while the students, now stirred to revolt themselves, do not even rise out of respect as custom would have dictated. Two full generations before the events of 1968, Gilles de Lointrain has discovered how easy it is to set free the frustrated energies of his contemporaries.

Like Denis Prullé-Rousseau in *Les Nouveaux Aristocrates* and Laurent de Balivière in *Laurent,* Gilles de Lointrain is in a state of revolt against society as a whole, and in particular against his own social class and its privileges. The very title of the novel, *Ce Monde ancien,* evokes this traditional class system against which the bourgeois hero hurls himself. Unsure of where he fits in, he rebels against the whole establishment. As the novel makes clear, the bourgeoisie in France is both a world unto itself as well as a part of a much larger system that includes other classes, and it is significant that at the outset of his career, Saint Pierre's bourgeois hero finds his salvation not in art but in hard work as a member of a lower class.

At the same time as Gilles is emblematic of the revolt of a young bourgeois male, René Le Steyr represents Saint Pierre's interest throughout his whole career in creating sympathetic working class characters who seek to become self-made men. Later on, in *Murmures de Satan,* Jean Dewinter, whose personal fortune will be made in the electronics business, will be one of the most successful of such characters both in terms of his level of affluence in the world and in the artistic detail with which he is created. Of course the other major proletarian hero created by Saint Pierre will be the priest, Abbé Paul Delance, whose life will be depicted in both *Les Nouveaux Prêtres* and its sequel *La Passion de l'abbé Delance.* Like Dewinter, he will harness his personal energies and work in harmony with divine grace to develop himself to the fullest as a person instead of allowing himself to be overwhelmed by the weight of circumstance and environment.

Le Steyr has spent the last four years as a laborer in the shipyards at Saint-Nazaire. His job responsibilities are limited and there is little likelihood of advancement in the future. Unlike a young bourgeois like Gilles who inherits from his family social contacts, class standing, and an open door to a university education, Le Steyr has inherited from his deceased parents nothing more than his grandfather's watch, and copies of the New Testament and of Marx's *Capital.* Although not necessarily a fast or brilliant thinker, he is a constant one, observing on all sides inefficient use of labor and machines. New, labor-saving devices are being sketched out in his mind, while at the same time he wonders why so many people perform tasks for which they are poorly paid when machines could perform the same work while making a better product at lower cost. This intelligent and industrious young man, although lacking a formal education, also chafes under the supervision of his foreman, Le Piquet. The reader, inevitably sharing his dissatisfaction with his life, cannot help but ask the same question that Le Steyr himself does: he cannot go on doing this forever, but what else is there? By the end of the novel he will be leaving for Paris to make his way in the world. Not sure of what he will eventually do, he knows that he can never return to the shipyards.

Gilles de Lointrain's revolt is symbolized by his interest in surrealism. He has begun writing poems and, in order to impose discipline on himself, is also keeping a diary. His classmate at the Sorbonne, Jacqueline Albertini, is the daughter of a woman who is the hostess of a literary salon that is reminiscent of that of Proust's Mme Verdurin. Featured among her regular guests are a certain Doctor Lannel, a lesbian couple, and assorted writers and intellectuals, all of whom have good connections and impressive academic and government appointments. Mme Albertini, however, takes a special interest in Gilles and invites him to her home, where she receives him in her bedroom. Discovering that he is still a virgin out of fidelity to unnamed principles, she invites him to sit beside her on her couch where she begins reading his poems aloud. Gilles, struck by the new life that she has given to his work, suddenly realizes that he is lying with his head in Mme Albertini's lap when Jacqueline comes home. He is embarrassed, but his hostess seems barely ruffled. As he gets up, she asks for permission to read his poems at the next meeting of her salon. "Non," he responds, "ne leur lisez pas mes vers, je vous en prie! Vous les avez trop bien lus aujourd'hui! Je ne veux rien oublier" (93).

The salon continues to be the central locus of his initiation into adulthood. Here he discusses with Dr. Lannel his interest in surrealism. But like many adolescents, he is better at expressing his true feelings and convictions to himself (in this case, in his diary) than in a public setting, for he is unable to rebut Dr. Lannel when the latter attacks surrealism as just another bourgeois fad. We find Gilles copying extracts from André Breton's writings in his diary, followed by his own naive comments. For instance, he writes, ecstatically: "Chère révolte, parfaite et vraie!" Or again: "André Breton, être admirable. Avec le style racinien qu'il a parfois, et cet accent péremptoire des prophètes inspirés. Joindre la vieille pureté de la langue française au ton le plus révolutionnaire, le plus neuf que nous ayons depuis Rimbaud!" (261). But on two occasions when he has the opportunity to defend surrealism, he becomes dumbstruck and unable to answer Dr. Lannel's rejection of the movement. To Lannel, "le surréalisme est l'art d'un monde sans culture" (56). It is a middle class gimmick which to him illustrates once again that "les classes moyennes sont parfaitement capables de se laisser prendre au piège d'un conformisme nouveau" (55-56). Despite the fact that some surrealists, adds Lannel, claim to be of proletarian origin and to be striving to create a new type of art for the working class, this is merely a facade, for surrealism is basically a form of bourgeois revolt and nothing more. "Je suis convaincu," he goes on, "pour ma part, que le surréalisme n'a aucune chance de réussir auprès du peuple. Le peuple est dans un monde en déclin le suprême refuge du bon sens" (p. 56). One thinks of Le Steyr, in revolt against his dreary proletarian existence in the shipyards, and it is difficult to imagine him taking surrealism seriously.

But while René Le Steyr continues to work within the stuctures of the prevailing economic system for the improvement of workers' rights (without becoming a member of the Communist Party), Gilles devotes his free time to writing a novel with the vision of surrealist revolt as his principal source of inspiration. Finally, he learns of an art exhibit that has been arranged to display the works of modern masters such as Duchamp, Dali, and Picasso. With his friend Auguste Lerat, he hurries off to get a close look at these examples of their work and is sadly disappointed by what he finds. As he confides to his diary, he returns to the exhibit once more, this time alone, to examine the paintings more closely, but now he concludes that

> le surréalisme est sans aucun doute la manifestation d'un grand effort dont il restera quelque chose. Mais après le rataplan glorieux des prophètes de l'art nouveau, quel bilan dérisoire! Je suis né trop tard ou trop tôt. Donc, on ne remplace pas Rembrandt—et cela me désespère. Brûlé le livre d'André Breton. (263-64)

Gilles has now moved beyond surrealism as a symbol and a motivating factor for his personal revolt. He knows that he wants to write and gradually he seems to be coming to the conclusion that his subject matter will have to be his own life and the things about which he has first-hand knowledge. Thus, we learn that he is taking segments of the diary and reworking them for insertion into the novel. He even goes so far as to read to his father the chapter in which his hero, Michel, tells his father why he is rebelling against society. Of course, his father laughs at him, while his mother, fortunately, is more consoling. Thus, the very fact that he is doing something as risky as writing a novel now becomes the essence of his revolt, and he no longer needs the shock value of surrealism to formalize that revolt. As an aspiring young novelist, the one thing that he lacks is a wider experience of life. He has a yearning to live more fully, to escape from the limitations, albeit privileged ones, of his bourgeois milieu. When he overhears two people talking about Action Catholique, the social movement of the interwar years in which lay people witnessed their faith to others in their social orbit, he becomes curious and decides to talk to a priest about it. This is a new idea and, to him: "Tout ce qui est nouveau console" (255).

The Abbé Meillard has been involved for years in the Jeunesses Ouvrières Chretiennes (JOC) and is thus a "jociste," but he thinks that the movement has perhaps gone too far. "Action du milieu sur le milieu, d'accord. Mais pourquoi cette action deviendrait-elle la seule valable? (255-56). Meillard is alarmed at the prospect of the rise of yet another "ism," in this case "ouvrièrisme." He tells Gilles: "Les réunions de jocistes n'assemblant que de jeunes ouvriers, s'égarent volontiers en une sorte de canonisation perpétuelle du prolétaire chrétien par lui-même" (256). But Gilles expresses yet another objection when he tells Meillard that the church should not place such emphasis on social and economic self-help schemes like this, but should concentrate first on the spiritual life of workers and attempt to uplift the souls of the unfortunate as a necessary first step. But Meillard, several generations in advance of our contemporary debate about "liberation theology," reminds him that a proletarian is someone who is essentially crushed by life and that "le peuple est éloigné, par sa condition même, de l'héroisme et de la sainteté" (257). One can only talk of spiritual matters, he claims, after one has fed the hungry and sheltered the cold and homeless. For this reason, "l'apostolat devient affreusement vain s'il ne s'appuie pas sur des préoccupations économiques et sociales" (257). Gilles is struck by this conversation and begins to suspect that the subject matter of his novel might be right here in the shadowy area in which the social and the religious intermingle. In fact, he seems to prefigure here Michel de Saint Pierre, whose future novels would also often reflect this same preoccupation, that is, the problem of living out the spirit of the gospels in the contemporary world. Finally, Gilles is so impressed by what the priest has told him that he confides to his diary that this conversation "donne mieux à penser que dix retraites et vingt sermons" (257).

At this point in Gilles's evolution to adulthood, he has come far enough through his period of revolt to realize that what he needs is a strong taste of the real world of work and responsibility. It is only here, forgetting himself in laborious routine, that he ironically will be able to find himself and discover whether or not he is meant to be a writer.

In the meantime, René Le Steyr has begun to attract the attention of the Communist Party because he has helped in organizing a weekly meeting to teach workers how to engage in public speaking. After the funeral of a fellow worker, he is approached by M. Ronat, the Party's chief organizer for the shipyards, and invited for lunch. Ronat, like the progressive priest, Fr. Barré in *Les Nouveaux Prêtres,* is a true "apôtre." He speaks with assurance, fervor, and conviction, whether in public, as he has just done at the deceased worker's grave site, or in private, as he will do during lunch with Gilles. As a trusted party organization man, Ronat is "épris d'un noble idéal, tourné vers un monde futur où la masse des travailleurs ne serait plus opprimée, où le peuple serait libre" (241). Since Le Steyr has a reputation among other workers as being a lucid and articulate analyst of working conditions, Ronat proposes that he continue to give his public speaking course, but do two additional things: eliminate the other person who has helped to organize the course, and attend the party meeting once a month to make an informal report. In exchange, he can expect to receive 1,000 F per month to remunerate him for his time. Le Steyr refuses the proposal, however, because it would mean that he would become nothing more than an informer who reports to the party on what other people say and do.

Several weeks later, Le Steyr is called to the office of the director, M. Boisgely. The latter, having been made aware of Le Steyr's successful "cours d'éloquence," is alarmed at some of the subjects that have been discussed, like paid vacations, work hours, and productive use of free time. Boisgely ironically proposes that Le Steyr continue his meetings, but that he allow his associate and fellow organizer of the meetings, Maurice de Saint-Apollon, the son of one of the company's engineers, to be replaced by a company representative and that he discuss the content of the meetings once a month with M. Boisgely himself. Once again, jealous of his independence, Le Steyr refuses an attractive offer, even at the risk this time of losing his job. But even as he makes this choice, it is clear that a price will have to be paid. This novel of initiation makes it clear that it is difficult for any young man, but especially one from a working class background, to maintain his independence while getting ahead in the world. If Le Steyr chooses to remain where he is, in the Saint-Nazaire shipyards, he will sooner or later have to take sides or be without a job.

This grim alternative becomes inevitable when, a few days later, René learns that a sketch that he made for a new bulkhead and given to an electrical engineer, M. Sellin, has been stolen by the latter, who has also applied for a patent on it. René is furious when he finds out what has happened. After work, he confronts Sellin and forces him, under threat of physical harm, to write a confession in which he describes in detail how he had adapted Le Steyr's ideas for his own ends. The next day René takes the confession to their supervisor, M. Moussard, who tells him that the confession is worthless. After all, how could he, René, without any formal education or training, come up with an idea that escaped the minds of the professionals, the electrical engineers with whom he worked? Obviously, there can only be one solution to the problem: René will have to leave. Having tried and failed to use physical force on M. Sellin to establish the truth about his own invention, and been tempted to prostitute himself by both the Communists and the shipyard owners, he must escape to an environment in which he can prove himself as an individual. Gilles's final break with his milieu is also triggered by his desire to assert his own individuality. It is only normal for adolescent friendships to dissolve as life's responsibilities call young men in different directions. Yet Gilles is especially upset at his friends' lack of any goal in life other than sticking together to make money and maintain their privileges. He goes over in his mind their chief characteristics: "volonté de jouissance; ambition médiocre . . . incompétence et hardiesse sur les plans artistiques et littéraires . . . prudence féroce partout ailleurs . . . conscience malléable" (314). When one of his friends tells Gilles that he is in love with him, this is the last straw, the ultimate in bourgeois decadence. Gilles refuses his advances and sees more clearly than ever his need to escape.

Interviewed about this book by André Bourin for *Les Nouvelles Littéraires,* Saint Pierre admitted that he had much in common with Gilles de Lointrain and in fact had copied whole sections from his diary into the novel. René Le Steyr, however, is more a product of his imagination and of the fifteen months that he spent working in the Saint-Nazaire shipyards before joining the Navy. As a novel of initiation, a *Bildungsroman,* it places its major emphasis on revolt, not so much against family as against the prevailing decadence of his bourgeois milieu in the thirties.

Published at a time when the Parisian literary vogue called for rather long, philosophical novels (Camus's *La Peste* had appeared the year before and Sartre was in the process of publishing the novels of the *Chemins de la liberté* series), *Ce Monde ancien* is also quite lengthy. Almost four hundred pages long, it is by far Saint Pierre's longest and most detailed novel. Interestingly, in retrospect, this was his only regret about the novel, that it was too long and "un peu prolixe." "Mon ideal," he told André Bourin, is to "faire court. Un des chefs d'œuvre français, c'est *Génitrix.* Pourtant, je n'aime pas Mauriac."[2] This quote is important because it announces an ideal that Saint Pierre would strive for in his future works: shorter novels, with a Catholic dimension to them, but without that trait that he always rejected in Mauriac's work: the absence of grace, the stifling atmosphere, the obsession with sexual guilt, and the emphasis on money and property as the principal determinants of human conduct. Saint Pierre could admire certain novels for specific reasons, as is the case with *Génitrix,* while rejecting—as a consciously Catholic writer himself—Mauriac's gloomy, even morbid, world view. By contrast, Saint Pierre characterized Bernanos in the same interview as "un grand bonhomme," and it would be clear in later works, especially in his three most "Catholic" novels, *Les Murmures de Satan, Les Nouveaux Prêtres,* and *La Passion de l'abbé Delance,* that he had a continuing debt to Bernanos the man and the writer.

Jean Mauduit, reviewing *Ce Monde ancien* in *Cahiers du Monde Nouveau,*[3] hailed the work as signalling the "naissance d'un écrivain," and correctly claimed that it confirmed Saint Pierre's "vocation de romancier." Still working part-time for a Parisian import/export firm and by now the father of two children, Saint Pierre needed encouragement and positive reaction to his work in order to make a full-time commitment to his writing.

La Mer à boire[4] (1951) is unique in Saint Pierre's fiction in so far as it is highly comical. As a novel of initiation, it deals with some of the same concerns expressed in *Ce Monde ancien,* but the tone and style are quite different. The anger and frustration of the two heroes of the earlier work have been replaced here by a tone of insouciance. This lighter touch is evidenced by the very title of the book. The French expression "ce n'est pas la mer à boire," can be roughly translated as "that's no difficult matter," or "that's no big deal." The title could thus be translated loosely as "Difficult Assignment" or "Big Deal" and it ironically pokes fun at this somewhat naive latter-day "chevalier" who cannot wait to prove—to himself especially—that he is a man.

Although sharing with Gilles de Lointrain a privileged background and a feeling of revolt against his caste, Marc Van Hussel is also quite different from him. In fact, much like Saint Pierre himself, Marc is enamored of sports, physical exertion, and athletic competition. He is also in love with the sea and the idea of adventure. He wants to find out about life by living it, not sitting idly by in the Sorbonne library and reading about it.

Marc's desire to rebel takes the form of insolence to his elders and superiors. Just as Gilles de Lointrain had provoked his history professor, M. Mothe, in front of the whole class, Marc, at the family dinner table, insults his uncle, a career officer in the French Navy, for being assigned to the Ministère de la Marine headquarters in Paris instead of being out at sea on a ship. Like Gilles, he is also interested in surrealism and devotes long hours in his room to painting canvases that evoke "le surréalisme et la pré-histoire," each one of which is "plein de cette bizarrerie qui fait partie du rêve moderne" (21-22). In other words, Marc is confused; he is mixed up. The value system that had prevailed for his parents has no validity for him. In place of a faith based on the law of charity found in Christian teachings, Marc has created for himself a faith and a rule of life based on the exploits of his pre-Christian, pagan Viking ancestors. He devotes long hours to reading the sagas that tell of their courageous deeds, and he dreams that one day he will be able to revel, like them, in the heat of battle. Marc thus joins the Navy to see the world and be ready for action when war comes. After several months he becomes a "maître d'hôtel" aboard ship and spends his days waiting on the officers at table, much like a young man of noble birth would have done in medieval times.

The novel is divided into five distinct sections, the first one ending with Marc's receiving a letter from Barbara, his girl friend, announcing the end of their relationship. As the second part begins, he is in Toulon, where he has joined the Navy over his parents' objections. Earning a mere 30 F per month, he has turned his back on medical school and the car that his father had promised him if he finished school. Still thinking of Barbara, he spends his free time on shore in bars and brothels.

Since Rémy Belfontaine, Barbara's new love interest, has been assigned to le Primauguet, the same ship as Marc, Barbara has come to live in Toulon in a villa owned by Rémy's mother. She wants to be near her fiancé, but at the same time she has not forgotten Marc. When she learns that Rémy has been assigned to the Far East for two and a half years, she asks him to talk to Marc in the hope that the latter will then respectfully leave her alone in Rémy's absence. Their conversation, at a café in Toulon and not aboard ship where Rémy is an officer and Marc the lowest ranking enlisted man, is highly comical. As Rémy earnestly beseeches Marc to be a good boy in his absence, Marc is only too happy to give him the assurances that he seeks, for he knows that Rémy will be gone in thirty days.

Although Marc is careful to keep away from Barbara until Rémy leaves, this does not mean that he lives a celibate life. In addition to availing himself of the prostitutes employed at the bordello run by la Grande Louise, he also meets Agnes Peterson, a Norwegian student temporarily in Toulon. They initiate a relationship that is purely erotic, without the complication of sentimental attachment. Their lovemaking scenes, discreetly rendered, and with the accent on the athletic and physically exhausting aspect of sex, are reminiscent of Céline more than of Mauriac or Bernanos. The third-person narrator tells us:

> Cette jeune femme était avide, musclée, sans autre mystère que sa perfection. Agnès dépensait une bonne volonté ingénieuse et calme. Elle se montra capable d'un effort soutenu. Vers cinq heures du matin, elle avait les yeux cernés mais son sourire demeurait confiant. 'Pas étonnant que ces gens-là gagnent les marathons,' songeait Marc, éreinté. (160)

In Marc's pre-Christian, pagan mind, Agnes is raised to the level of a goddess because of her sexual exploits: "Elle est éternelle. J'ai rencontré la déesse, la déesse brute," he says to himself as he makes love to her (160).

While Marc is in the process of accumulating erotic experiences and learning about Navy life, we intermittently hear in the background radio news reports about the latest events on the diplomatic front. Hitler and his cohorts are generally feared by most people who hear these reports and discuss them with Marc, for they do not want war—especially in a Navy town like Toulon. But for Marc, each newscast raises his hopes that the outbreak of war will soon be announced. He tells la Grande Louise that he has enlisted for no other reason than that he wants to be aboard ship and ready for combat on that fateful day and not have to wait to be called up as a reservist. Like his Scandinavian ancestors (Marc, like Saint Pierre, is proud of his Norman heritage), whose exploits he has read about so many times in the ancient sagas, and whose physical abilities are perpetuated in modern-day Scandinavian goddesses like Agnes Peterson, Marc wants to prove himself in war. Nothing less will satisfy him.

As the fifth and last section of the novel begins, Marc's ship has undergone necessary repairs and is getting ready to go to sea. At the same time, Rémy Belfontaine has gone off to Indochina, leaving Barbara alone in Toulon. In its closing pages, the novel rushes to its denouement. While waiting somewhat impatiently for war to be declared, Marc's temper runs a bit high and he becomes embroiled in a vicious brawl with other sailors from his own ship. The incessant waiting in the last days of the "phony war" only exacerbates the thirst for blood and desire for violence that these young men display. At the same time, Barbara represents a final challenge because Marc too will have to leave Toulon. War or no war, his ship will be ready within a few weeks.

After this last brawl, Marc is badly beaten and wanders by Barbara's villa in the middle of the night. She takes him in and treats his wounds. They spend the rest of the night together in bed, but cannot make love—despite Barbara's willingness—because Marc is too exhausted. Before going to sleep, he tells her that he has finally given up on France and her Navy and has decided to desert the next day: the politicians have been too successful in avoiding war and in giving Hitler everything he wants. When he awakens the next day about noon, he is feeling better and his amorous instincts have returned. Barbara shares his feelings, but when she tells him that word has just come over the radio that war has been declared, he takes leave and hurries off to his ship. As the novel ends, civilians are rushing about the streets of Toulon in excited confusion and fear about the German invasion of Poland, while Marc, delighted, hurries back to *Le Primauguet*.

In both subject matter and its treatment, this is not, strictly speaking, a Catholic novel. At the same time, however, the metaphysical and spiritual dimension of the story is not to be overlooked, for Marc is not unaware of the validity and importance of spiritual questions. He has merely decided to defer making decisions about them.

> A l'égard de la vie spirituelle et des choses de la religion, il avait choisi la neutralité provisoire. . . . il remettait à plus tard le moment de décider si, oui ou non, il chercherait Dieu. Le besoin de se trouver soi-même, de se réaliser dans la violence, le submergeait. (215)

Here at the beginning of a long career as a professional writer, Saint-Pierre is giving us what is in effect his second autobiographical novel. It depicts another aspect of the author's character, transformed in part but still largely intact, at the beginning of his own adulthood and of World War II. The more sensitive, artistically inclined side of Saint Pierre's character is revealed in the character of Gilles de Lointrain, while the fun-loving, mischievous side comes across in Marc Van Hussel.

Luc Estang compared the novel favorably to the works of Pierre Loti and Claude Farrère and noted that it was "nourri par un documentaire détaillé et sans nul doute exact sur la marine française."[5] He was especially struck by Saint Pierre's ability to tell the story from the sailor's and not from the officer's point of view. Emile Henriot had a similar reaction:

M. Michel de Saint Pierre a beaucoup de verve. Il fait très vivant, et son livre, un peu lent d'abord, se lit par la suite avec amusement, entre ses coups de brise marine, ses bonnes buffes, ses dialogues militaires et ses virées nocturnes dans le Toulon d'avant l'horrible destruction.[6]

Paul Guth was especially struck by the idea of service to one's country that emerges from the novel. Noting Marc's revolt against bourgeois conformity and comfort, he hailed the young hero's willingness to take risks in order to make himself a better person. "Mais l'essentiel est la notion de service," he wrote. "Ce Marc brutal et dégoûté, impatient de toute discipline, blasé et revenu de tout, aspire à la guerre. Non pour tuer, mais obscurément, pour se purifier par le don de soi."[7] Guth goes on to hail the work as one that courageously goes against the prevailing existentialist fashion of the day: "Les jeunes gens que nous montre le roman contemporain, se vautrent, en général, dans l'alcool et la veulerie. Ils s'adonnent à la pornographie et aux mots gras. L'existentialisme, il faut le reconnaître, a beaucoup contribué à cette esthétique de l'avachissement." In contrast, he finds *La Mer à boire* to be "un roman athlétique, tout en muscles et en détentes. Michel de Saint Pierre le mène en 26 petits rounds rigoureusement troussés." As a result, he was in Guth's opinion "un des auteurs les plus éclatants de sa génération."

In conclusion, *La Mer à boire* and *Ce Monde ancien* present two divergent sides of an emerging author's personality and fictionalize his life experience as a young man in two different, but complementary, ways. Already known as a Catholic writer for his regular contributions to two Catholic periodicals, *Témoignage Chrétien* and *Cahiers du Monde Nouveau,* he was now trying to find his way as a novelist. Although both Gilles and Marc come from traditional Catholic backgrounds, neither of these works can be called a Catholic novel. Each is primarily a *Bildungsroman* with the emphasis on the process of self-discovery, and not on the drama of salvation.

3. Moving Beyond the Autobiographical Novel

LES ARISTOCRATES[1] (1954) WAS SAINT PIERRE'S FIRST GREAT commercial success, being translated into a half dozen languages. In addition, it was also a *succès d'estime*. As Emile Henriot put it, writing in *Le Monde:* "S'il ne dépendait que de moi, je lui décernerais d'un seul coup tous les prix littéraires disponibles, le Goncourt et le Fémina, le Renaudot et le Prix du roman de l'Académie. Cela simplifierait beaucoup le travail des jurys de décembre, et le grand public serait content d'un bon choix et d'un livre gai"[2]. The novel deals with an aristocratic family presided over by the Marquis de Maubrun. A widower for the past fifteen years and the father of seven children, six boys and a girl, Maubrun lives on his rural family estate in Burgundy and bears several traits in common with members of Saint Pierre's family, although there is enough adaptation of known biographical material to make the work truly fictional. Born and raised in a noble provincial family in Normandy, Saint Pierre transposes the action to Burgundy, but he is still writing from the inside. He knows what he is talking about here. It should also be recalled that Saint Pierre's cousin, Henri de Montherlant, had also devoted a novel, *Les Célibataires* (1934), to this subject, but the latter's treatment, a cruel and biting satire, does not take the same approach as does Saint Pierre's book, which is more ironic and bittersweet toward his material. At the same time as he gives credit to Maubrun's sense of loyalty and of service to others, he also pokes fun at his inability to come to terms with postwar reality.

Like Bernanos, Saint Pierre is nostalgic for the middle ages, a period when, to his mind, there still flourished the spirit of chivalry, that is, a willingness to sacrifice oneself in the service of the poor and the power-less without asking anything in return and in which money, always important to human life, was still secondary, being subordinated to spiritual values. Bernanos often referred to Joan of Arc as a symbol of this other age and of what he took to be its ethos. Saint Pierre, however, takes a some-what different approach. Instead of looking back in time, he prefers to deal with the chivalrous ideal in its contemporary context.

As in Saint Pierre's family, the Maubrun children have inherited the blood of a lesser form of nobility through their mother. Since Maubrun had married the descendant of a certain Maréchal Mosquet du Hodna, who had won his title of baron during the 1830s for his military exploits, the question arises at the very beginning of the novel as to whether this type of nobility, going back only for several generations, and in any case not as far back as the Old Regime, is valid or not. Like Saint Pierre's father, the his-torian Louis de Saint Pierre, who wrote a good deal about his own wife's ancestor, Marshall Soult, who distinguished himself at Austerlitz with Napoleon and later served the Bourbons under the Restoration, the brother-in-law of the Marquis de Maubrun is writing the life of the "maréchal inconnu," as the fictional Maréchal du Hodna is called. As we shall see below, in a world which no longer recognizes hereditary nobility, preferring to think in terms of a modern meritocracy, such quibbling seems out of place. If, in the end, Maubrun's children have no trouble taking the "maré-chal inconnu" as a legitimate nobleman, they do not seem to give the matter much thought. Their father, however, continues to be vexed by it and is delighted when, toward the end of the book, his brother-in-law and family genealogist, M. de Lointrain,[3] is able to locate more noble forebears for the "maréchal inconnu."

At the same time, a line regarding what is and what is not nobility seems to be more clearly drawn in the case of the Maubruns' neighbor, the Baron de Conti. Conti, an upright bachelor of forty years of age, has received his title from his father, who started out in life as an ironworker and, through a series of social maneuvers, acquired the title Baron de Conti. He is in love with Daisy, now in her mid-twenties, as she is with him. At first, because of their father's strong resistance to Conti, the six brothers do not seem to take very seriously the possibility of marriage between their sister and Conti. But then, as they get to know him, their indifference is transformed into approval, and they attempt to persuade their father that there is nothing wrong with this relationship. But when Maubrun resists and forbids Daisy to ever see Conti again, she runs away from home for several days, staying at Conti's estate. Sadly, Daisy returns, agreeing to break off with Conti in exchange for her father's never asking what has taken place between her and her would-be lover.

In the meantime, Daisy's friend Jeanne, a young woman she has met in Paris, has come to spend the end of the summer with the family. In fact, it is this vacation period that also allows two of the six brothers to also be at Maubrun: Arthus, also called "le Turc," who is temporarily on leave from his job in Istanbul, where he has made a great deal of money, and Philippe, a Jesuit priest taking a rest before leaving for Africa as a missionary. Slowly, the Marquis falls in love with Jeanne, or at least deludes himself into thinking that he is in love with this woman who wants to become his wife. But his children, ironically, encourage him to resist. They had been willing to allow their sister to marry the Baron de Conti, despite his doubtful nobility, because they were convinced that to do so was a reasonable decision, since Conti himself is such a fine person. But when it comes to having an outsider like Jeanne become their stepmother (a woman who, despite the thirty-year age difference between herself and the Marquis, still hopes to get her way), all the children, especially Daisy, stand united against her. Thus, although they are all much better adapted to the modern world and its theoretical egalitarianism, they cannot envision an outsider of much lower rank usurping their privileges and clouding their inheritance. It is on this bittersweet note, with Jeanne leaving the château in the face of the massive opposition of Maubrun's children, that the novel ends.

Henri de Montherlant liked the book and described its subject matter as follows:

> Votre sujet est ceci: la loi du clan se retourne contre celui qui l'exerçait le premier. Le marquis se refuse à ce que sa fille épouse un 'rôturier'.... Ses enfants, à leur heure, feront bloc pour qu'il n'épouse pas une 'rôturière,' qu'il aime, et qui de surcroît a une vocation d'infirmière, ce qui a son prix car le marquis est cardiaque: perisse le papa plutôt que les principes.[4]

Montherlant's résumé of the plot is a fair one and it does distill quite well the main irony of the novel. Yet it leaves aside another related aspect of the theme of nobility and its relationship to the idea of aristocracy. In other words, to Saint Pierre, the two words are not synonymous and he does not want his reader to assume that all noblemen are aristocrats and vice versa. To this end, the novel seems to be attempting to show a number of areas in which the two terms overlap, as well as those in which they have different meanings.

On a number of occasions during his career, at the time of publication of *Les Aristocrates,* as well as, sporadically, later on, Saint Pierre has made the distinction between the "noblesse" and the "aristocratie" in France. The former are simply the group of families who are able to prove to the satisfaction of the "commission des preuves" of the Association de la Noblesse Française that their pedigree is suitably "noble." The other category, however, the "aristocrats," are, etymologically speaking, "the best" that any society can produce. The distinction, both by definition and by Saint Pierre's personal yardstick, is that someone can be a true "aristocrat" because of his personal value as an individual human being, even though, because of lack of pedigree, he or she is not "noble."

During the Old Regime, it was possible for a man to enter the nobility through the purchase of his title, so that the ranks of the nobility were forever expanding to allow entry of "the best" of commoners into society's elite. Since the Revolution, or rather, since Napoleonic times, one can no longer enter the aristocracy since it has ceased to exist officially as a class in a supposedly egalitarian society. But, contends Saint Pierre, there are still many worthy individuals in our mass, impersonal society, who possess those outstanding traits of courage, intelligence, loyalty, and integrity that, in an earlier day, when allied with wealth, would have allowed them to enter the nobility. But this transformation of a commoner into a member of the nobility could only take place because he or she was already, in terms of personal worth, an "aristocrat," one of the best. Since this is no longer possible, Saint Pierre wants to investigate here the relationship between those who are born into the "noblesse," but who are not necessarily aristocrats until they have proven themselves, and those who have proven themselves in life to be "aristocrats," even though by heredity they do not belong to the noble caste. Looking back on Saint Pierre's first two novels, it is obvious that both Gilles de Lointrain and René Le Steyr of *Ce Monde ancien* are aristocrats in terms of their personal value as people. They represent the best of their generation in their particular milieu. Later on, Fabre-Simmons of *Le Milliardaire* and Doctor Erickson of the novel by the same name, will also be aristocrats. As Saint Pierre said repeatedly over the years: "Je ne donne pas à la noblesse le privilège exclusif de l'aristocratie."[5]

When asked by his nephew to describe the relationship between his private life of faith and his political vision and multiple activities in the political domain, Charles de Gaulle is said to have answered: "Je suis catholique par l'histoire et la géographie."[6] Likewise, the Maubrun family of the novel are Catholics by the weight of tradition: since they are both French and aristocrats, they cannot possibly be anything else. Although just as De Gaulle's answer to his nephew can be read as an evasive one in which he seems to be avoiding a deeper discussion of the relationships involved, *Les Aristocrates* does investigate the connection between traditional adherence to Catholicism and the French aristocratic tradition. First of all, the Marquis is a truly hereditary Catholic in De Gaulle's sense. His faith is simple: it does not make room for deep speculation, nor does it keep him from doing what he wants, even though his conduct is in direct contradiction to prescribed morality. For instance, he is delighted to serve at his son Philippe's daily mass and is truly solicitous about the welfare of a neighbor in a state of severe financial distress. Yet he has a mistress in Paris whom he visits from time to time and is largely incapable of acting charitably toward his daughter, Daisy. At the same time, Jeanne, who is an atheist, is in many ways the kindest, noblest, and most charitable character in the novel. If she wants to marry the Marquis, it is because she is truly in love with him. As a nurse, she seeks in life to create happiness around her. Her goal is a modest one, and she appears to be completely without pretense. When she discusses with the Marquis what to do about Daisy, who has been temporarily banished from the château, she advises him to take her back, thus exposing his coldhearted and uncharitable attitude toward his daughter in the name of abstract principle: "Quand un être est blessé," she tells him, "on ne marche pas dessus. On le relève. Même s'il s'agit de sa propre fille—même s'il faut se baisser un peu. Voilà ce que j'aimerais vous dire, si j'étais Dieu" (168). Untouched by grace and without faith, her persistent good sense and simple charity contrast sharply with the Marquis's intolerance and stubbornness.

It is Philippe, however, who in the most consistent fashion raises the question of the relationship between faith and modern life. A decorated veteran of World War II, he is, like Loyola, both a soldier and an aristocrat. Of all the boys, he is the one we get to know best, and we will meet him again in *Les Nouveaux Aristocrates*. To him, happiness can only be found in modern life through a cultivation of detachment. He keeps a thick note-book that he carries around with him. In it, he writes down quotations that have touched or affected him. He is sure of his vocation, but uncertain that he should be going off to Chad, as planned at the end of the summer, as a missionary. He feels unequal to the challenge: "Je suis indigne de prêcher l'Evangile aux Noirs," he writes. "Indigne de leur annoncer Jésus-Christ. J'aurais pu être un bon petit prof de Math-Elem dans une boîte de Jésuites en France. Au lieu de cela, je suis la voie qu'on devrait réserver aux Saints" (137). He is a realist who is aware that there are many problems in France that cry out for solutions, including the need for more social justice and a wider spirit of egalitarianism. When he expresses this opinion to his father while telling him that Daisy ought to be allowed to marry Conti, his father accuses him of being a "prêtre progressiste" (242) who has been unduly influenced by modern ideas emanating from the Action Catholique move-ment. When the son responds that his father's ideas are nothing but "préjugés ridicules" (243), his father offers his ultimate defense of the aristocracy as the nation's most disinterested servants:

> Sais-tu combien il reste en France de familles authentiquement nobles? A peine quatre mille, Philippe. Ce qui fait trente ou quarante mille personnes en tout. Et jamais tu ne pourras imaginer, mesurer leur importance. Elles veulent absolument se faire tuer à toutes les guerres. Elles ont un goût contagieux pour des choses qui semblent inutiles. Que te dire encore? Elles ont à la fois la tentation de mépriser et le goût de servir. Partout où elles sont, Philippe, le niveau monte. Tu ne vois pas, toi, cette petite armée de bougres à beaux noms qui marchent sur toute l'épaisseur de l'histoire et des traditions? Je m'en vais te prédire une bonne chose, l'abbé: quand la France aura perdu ces gens-la, elle sera morte. (245-46)

Understood in the Marquis's argument, of course, is the idea that the aristocracy is a Christian phenomenon and that he and his sons are latter-day knights whose idea of service springs from a divine source. Faith and service to the nation are linked, with the hereditary aristocrat serving as the symbol of this bond. Philippe, who cannot go along completely with his father's ideas, is unable to respond. The tension that results from this lack of communication is at the heart of the novel: the clash of old, and (to the

Marquis) proven traditional values, against the need to renew and adapt them if they are to be able to endure.

Saint Pierre pokes fun at his noblemen in a number of ways. Despite his apparent sympathy for them, and for what they have meant to French society over the centuries, they are not immune to his barbs. As mentioned above, we find at the very heart of the novel the ironic question of whether or not an ancestor several generations removed, the "maréchal," is really an "aristocrat" even though he was raised to that exalted level only in the first half of the nineteenth century. He plays up this intra-family argument magnificently, for Maubrun, ever faithful to what he takes to be the purity of aristocratic traditions, cannot admit that someone elevated to the aristocracy at a relatively recent date, despite his personal achievements and worth as a person, can be compared to someone born into the aristocracy.

Of the many scenes in the novel that ridicule certain aspects of aristocratic pretention, one stands out in particular. On one of his visits to Paris, the Marquis has been called to meet Don Felipe, a Spanish descendant of Louis XIV and at present a monarchical pretender without a throne. Maubrun is received ceremoniously at the Hôtel Crillon in the Place de la Concorde where they engage in superficial conversation for an hour. Finally, Don Felipe, who could never imagine speaking any other language but French while he is in Paris, gets around to telling him why he has called: he would like to take a vacation in October and has decided to invite himself to Maubrun's château. Of course, the Marquis is delighted at this opportunity and tells him that he will be lodged in the Chambre du Roi. When Don Felipe asks how the room got its name, Maubrun tells him that it was once prepared to receive Louis XIV in 1685—but that the Sun King, unfortunately, never appeared. The irony of a penurious and impoverished pretender to a nonexistent throne attempting to arrange a low budget vacation in the Chambre du Roi where no king has ever slept is biting. The scene is typical of one of the novel's great strengths.

A much deeper questioning of the aristocracy's mode of existence and chances for survival is depicted through the string of contrasts upon which the novel is built, a series that can perhaps be summed up as a clash between the "old" and the "new." On the side of the "old," of the backward-looking sense of tradition, we find, first of all, the castle itself. From the beginning to the very end of the novel, its preservation and up-keep will be a key issue. It is several hundred years old, dating back to the late middle ages. It was built in an age when the idea of progress had not yet come into existence. The foundations of its massive walls are sunk deep into the Burgundian soil and, as added protection against outsiders, it is surrounded by a moat. Despite its present fall from grace, it is "trapue, au-dessus du paysage, arrogante et crénelée" (4). Its walls might give much evidence of wear and tear, but to M. de Maubrun, that is only another good reason to plug up these fissures, no matter what financial sacrifices must be made in order to do so. The *château de Maubrun* stands throughout the novel as an enduring symbol of the aristocracy, with the two twins, Osmond and Louis-César residing at one end of the building in the Tour Brunehaut, aging Tante Mathilde in the Tour du Nord, and the servants at the other end of the building in the Tour du Midi. Inside the castle, looking backward in time with M. de Maubrun, are the two old aunts, Tante Corysande and Tante Mathilde. Around and about them are scattered ancient pieces of furniture, tapestries, and oil paintings—each one a reminder of the past, of the ancestors who acquired them, of what they have done and where they have been. Finally, on the side of tradition we must also include the very manner in which M. de Maubrun takes his leisure, hunting, which is portrayed as nothing more than a domesticated form of warfare, the chief pastime of his medieval ancestors.

On the side of the "new" are, first of all, the twins. They are forever playing jokes on Tante Corysande, lighting firecrackers outside her window, and blaring the raucous sounds of their radio in close proximity to ears not accustomed to enduring such intrusions. The boys also speak to each other in a form of slang that contrasts with the more precise and standardized medium of their elders. I might add, that Saint Pierre's attentive ear captures this slang faithfully. Emile Henriot has characterized the twins as "le couple impayable enfin des deux derniers-nés, frères jumeaux, Osmond et Louis-César, dont les plaisants méfaits et l'argot savoureux, dans le plus moderne goût du jour, égaient le livre d'un bout à l'autre."[7] He might have added that the twins, precisely in so far as they are the youngest Maubrun children, coming of age during the post World War II period with all of its American influences, are the means by which the novel can ask where French youth—not only aristocratic youngsters—are headed. As in Saint Pierre's other novels that deal in detail with the difficult adolescent period, the answer is not a happy one: American influences, as represented by rock music and chewing gum, a lack of respect for traditional ways of speaking and dressing, are driving these youngsters away from their traditions. The reader senses that the ethos of egalitarianism will play a much greater role in their lives than in those of the older siblings or, surely, their father.

The other children, especially Daisy and M. de Maubrun's oldest son Arthus, nicknamed "le Turc," also represent this new way of looking at life. Daisy, in love with the Baron de Conti as a person, even though he is not an "aristocrat" in the eyes of her father, and Arthus, adept at making money, even though he springs from a long line of Frenchmen for whom nothing could be more vulgar, represent these new values. As might be expected, the four older boys all served in the Resistance during the occupation as well as in the French First Army at the end of the war, but since then only one of them, Gontran, the second oldest, has been unable to adapt to the new postwar realities. Without a job, and uninterested in looking for one, he spends his days working about the castle, repairing and rebuilding as his father's funds will allow. Edouard, the most poetically inclined of the boys, spends a great deal of time reading and, presumably, writing. He is bored by hunting and other aristocratic rituals and has learned how to balance his own personal budget by buying and selling used cars in Paris.

The Marquis's quaint obsolescence is highlighted when, toward the end of the novel, Arthus suggests that the best way to save the castle, which urgently needs repairs that his father cannot pay for, is to form a corporation that he will get off the ground with a loan of several million francs. As might be expected, his father's reaction is totally negative. Rather than do that, he will decide to sell off his last two horses as well as two antique rifles. It is easier for the Marquis to dispose of these symbols of his caste than to compromise himself in a financial deal that he is incapable of understanding. Here, as the novel closes, the narrator's bittersweet ironic voice describes Maubrun as he tries to drive from his mind the thought of what he is doing: "Il ne voulait pas réfléchir, mesurer le présent ni peser l'avenir. Si tout le reste l'abandonnait, le château serait son témoin. 'Pour témoigner devant qui?' murmura M. de Maubrun en fermant son livre de comptes" (348). Thus, despite the narrator's sympathetic portrayal of the aristocracy, notably in the lively discussion between Maubrun and his son, the young Jesuit, Philippe, on the value of the aristocracy to French society, the novel ends on a note of irony that allows the author to back off from a simple acceptance of the aristocracy's claims to superiority. If society has changed so much that the castle, as the living symbol of a caste and its ideal that are no longer widely accepted, is not worth keeping up, then Maubrun is a fool to make such enormous sacrifices to preserve it. But so be it, Saint

Pierre seems to be saying. In an egalitarian society, everyone cannot be expected to understand what the castle means in terms of French history and traditions. But that is precisely one aspect of the aristocrat's vocation: to keep alive such values, even in the face of the laughter of one's uncomprehending contemporaries.

The ultimate irony of the novel is reflected in the artful manner in which the roles of Daisy and Jeanne are reversed at the denouement. Jeanne, while supporting Daisy in her relationship with Conti, seemed at first to be flirting with Gontran, but when Daisy returns home on condition that her father never inquire about the nature of her physical relationship with Conti, Jeanne seems to be more interested in the Marquis than in his son. When it becomes clear that she is in love with the Marquis, with whom she has interceded to facilitate Daisy's return home, it is Daisy who leads the opposition and successfully mobilizes her brothers against her. Daisy, who only yesterday was willing to make a marriage with someone whose social rank was below what her father thought appropriate for her, now keeps her father from doing the same thing. At the close of the novel, as the Marquis sits at his ledger books and contemplates the sale of his beloved horses and rifles, Jeanne is wandering off through the woods. Broken and defeated, she is leaving the Maubruns. She does not belong.

The success of *Les Aristocrates* made Saint Pierre's name a household word almost overnight in France. The following year, when the film version of the novel appeared, starring Pierre Fresnay (who had played the legendary Capitaine de Boïeldieu in Jean Renoir's *La Grande Illusion* in the thirties), that success was compounded. Interestingly, critical reaction to the novel focused on the book's apparent simplicity and limpid style. Kléber Haedens wrote:

> Alors que beaucoup de romanciers présentent leurs personnages d'une façon confuse et qu'il faut lire des pages et des pages avant de s'y retrouver, Michel de Saint Pierre se fait le champion de la clarté. Il n'oblige pas son lecteur à se poser des questions inutiles et son livre ne se perd pas dans les détails. . .[8]

Likewise, Yves Gandon pointed out that its power comes from its attention to everyday life without artifice. He hailed it as a "livre preste, pimpant, joyeux, mélancolique, et, sans faiblesse ni affectation, modelé sur la vie. L'intrigue ne rebondit pas en péripéties compliquées."[9]

During the many interviews that followed the success of *Les Aristocrates,* Saint Pierre was asked repeatedly what his aims were as a writer. He answered:

> J'ai une conception spéciale—et même idéale—du roman. Il me semble qu'il doit brasser un grouillement d'êtres comme la vie elle-même; qu'il doit être marqué du rythme alterné de la souffrance et de la joie—comme la vie! Je le voudrais de bonne foi, c'est-à-dire sans thèse; je désirerais aussi qu'il soit prophétique: le romancier peut recueillir l'avenir épars autour de lui et l'annoncer.[10]

In looking back at his first three novels from the perspective of the post-publication success of *Les Aristocrates,* we can see that Saint Pierre was in fact successful in creating a thriving universe reflecting life's frustrations and complexities. In addition, his sense of ironic distance from his characters, his ability to seem to agree with so many of the things that they believe in and strive after, while at the same time gently poking fun at them, indicates his success in writing what can in no sense be called thesis novels. Finally, the prophetic element that he claimed to be striving for is a new element in his *ars poetica,* one that will grow in importance as his career progresses. Later, it will be seen that the lay community of *Les Murmures de Satan* offers a foretaste of so many of the post-Vatican II experimental communities, that the spiritual anguish of bourgeois teenagers presented in *Les Nouveaux Aristocrates* predicts obliquely the events of 1968 and that the crisis within French Catholicism delineated in *Les Nouveaux Prêtres* presages greater crises and more extensive confusion in the Church's identity.

Although I agree with Emile Henriot that "le livre est des plus réussis, vivant, entraînant, plein de talent à chaque page,"[11] I must also admit that its Catholic dimension is not readily apparent and was barely noticed at the time. However, Saint Pierre's religious convictions are imbedded in the text insofar as the Marquis de Maubrun and his clan are representative of a certain type of French Catholicism. After the success of *Les Aristocrates,* Saint Pierre had not yet completely discovered his vocation as a Catholic novelist. That would come several years later.

Les Ecrivains,[12] built around the conflict between order and tradition on the one hand, and self-indulgence and novelty on the other, deals principally with the generational struggle between Alexandre Damville, an established writer in his sixties who budgets every minute of his day in order to grind out books and articles, and his son Georges, a young man of twenty-five with literary talent and high aspirations but as yet no successes, who drinks too much, stays out too late, and wastes too much of his time on passing fads.

As in *Les Aristocrates,* one often gets the impression that the setting of the scene, the painting of the tableau, the description of daily habits, and the nuances of language, are more important than the story line itself. Of course, the two are bound up together, but the narration in a sense can be said to be subordinate to the deeper reality of the private world of the professional writer of great genius in which Alexandre Damville moves. Also, despite Saint Pierre's prefatory remarks to the effect that this novel is not a *roman à clé* and that "pas un seul de ces personnages n'est un portrait, que chacun d'eux est le fruit de mon imagination" (11), it is nonetheless obvious that the great Damville has been fashioned after Saint Pierre's distant cousin, Henri de Montherlant.

Damville is now sixty-two years old and the author of some thirty books, including twenty novels and four plays. This vast production is described by his son as "une œuvre païenne de moraliste, austère, insolente" (225), and in order to achieve it the elder Damville has imposed a stoic discipline on himself. Since he does not believe in an afterlife, the body of work that he will leave behind will have to constitute his claim to immortality. He rejects fads or trends, whether in literature, dress, or social comportment. Instead, he sees himself as a kind of bridge linking past and future generations. In contrast, Georges, not yet sure of what he wants to say, but ardently wishing to express something of value, is distracted by novelties and fads, spends too much time at parties, and generally wastes his time, energy, and talent. Thus, the characters can be said to incarnate the deeper structures of French intellectual life, built as it is on the creative tension between "classic" and "romantic," "tradition" and "experimentation," "ancients" and "moderns." From this conflict, new ideas and forms emerge on the surface of reality, but the deeper antagonisms endure.

Saint Pierre also explores the problem of religious faith in this novel. He does so through the introduction of two female characters, neither one of whom, unfortunately, is ever completely drawn. The first of the two, Yvonne Lebrun, is present in Alexandre Damville's life throughout the novel, and her letters to him play a role in what might in fact be his salvation as the novel ends. A frustrated writer, Yvonne is a middle-aged woman whom Damville meets at a dinner party. She tells him that she has read all of his books, but disapproves of the bitter pessimism that characterizes several of them. When he asks if she is a Catholic, she responds: "Catholique, oui, Catholique pratiquante" (125), and when he inquires what the difference might be between a "Catholic" and a "practicing Catholic," she affirms: "La première est catholique et la seconde ne l'est pas. Voilà" (125). Damville responds sardonically that he is not surprised to hear this, since in many religions the rites and rituals often become ends in themselves: "J'ai noté," he tells her, "que la pratique est en effet l'essentiel des religions. La forme prime le fond. Et cela n'a rien qui puisse étonner, s'agissant d'un ensemble de rites et de cérémonies qui entourent le dieu inventé comme un rempart entoure une ville" (125). But Lebrun disagrees strongly: "Non, Monsieur. Vous n'y avez rien compris du tout. Pour nous, il ne s'agit pas de forme, comme vous dites. Il s'agit de la messe et des sacrements. Et c'est là que le mystère commence." But then, when their conversation is interrupted as they are called to the dinner table, she adds: "Oui, je doute que vous soyez de bonne foi sur le chapitre de la religion. Vous avez toujours eu la terreur d'être choisi" (126). Although Yvonne and the elder Damville will never meet again, the channels of communication will remain open through their correspondence.

The other character who raises the issue of faith is Damville's mistress, the widow Eve Chambleau. Without children, she seems willing to play the role of stepmother to Georges and hopes that he will accept her. But his only desire is to somehow avenge his mother's memory by insulting Eve. When she tells him that she is a believing Catholic and yet continues her love affair with the elder Damville, Georges explodes: "Je ne comprends pas. Vous croyez en Dieu, et vous n'êtes même pas fichu de diriger votre vie dans le sens de votre foi?" (165). She then admits to him: "Non, je n'en suis pas capable! Dieu est exigeant, mais l'amour est aussi exigeant que lui. Je . . . Je crois en effet que j'ai fini par diviniser votre père" (166).

It is apparent that Saint Pierre wanted to impart a metaphysical and religious dimension to the novel and that these two characters were the chief means of achieving that end. They are thinly depicted, however, and we barely get to know them. In the case of Eve Chambleau, her interesting conversation with Georges Damville speaks for itself. It is difficult to believe that her faith means very much to her. Her willingness to let herself be manipulated and humiliated by him indicates that, if anything, her problems are psychological in nature and not related to her faith.

She is on target, however, when she admits that she has deified Damville. Although he is not quite a god in objective terms, he is something quite close to it in cultural terms: a high priest of Literature. As such, the most precious commodity at his disposal is his time, of which he will never have enough if he is to leave behind him a suitable monument both to himself and to Literature. He has already neglected his deceased wife, Georges's mother, who seems to have died as much from depression and neglect as from anything else, and he prefers to give as little of himself to others, including (and perhaps especially) Eve, as he possibly can. Thus, her willingness to be available to him even though she knows that he is not even faithful to her raises a question about her common sense and psychological balance. As a result, the issue of faith as it is raised through the character of Eve never really becomes compelling. Eve will eventually become submerged in the novel as yet another female, Marguerite Villère, a young actress starring in Damville's latest play, attracts his attention. It is frustration over Marguerite's rejection of his advances and her preference for Georges that will lead to his death of a stroke.

Damville does not die immediately after being stricken. Several hours pass during the middle of the night as he gazes upon an envelope containing the latest letter from Yvonne Lebrun. In their previous meeting and in her first subsequent letter to him, Yvonne had attempted to make clear to Damville her conviction that as a creative writer of great talent, he is participating in God's work of creation. She recognizes that in hoarding his time in order to devote himself entirely to his *œuvre,* he feels justified in referring to himself sternly as an egoist, but she disagrees with this assessment. To her, the very fact that he harnesses his powers and avoids distractions in order to write means that he is seeking a higher level of communication:

> Pour écrire, vous êtes prêt à renoncer au genre humain, à l'abandonner totalement. Et cependant, c'est pour lui que vous composez votre œuvre à laquelle vous avez tout sacrifié. Le maître-égoïste est celui qui, parvenu à votre âge, à votre degré de célébrité (le haut de l'échelle), renoncerait à écrire. D'ailleurs, l'un des actes irrémédiablement condamnés par le Christ est celui d'enfouir le talent.

Thus, Yvonne concludes that despite Damville's avowed atheism, there is still a sense in which his work can be called Christian: "Vous rejoignez

ainsi le monde chrétien chaque fois que vous 'lancez' vos livres. . ."
(180).

As he lies in bed, paralyzed and unable to speak or to call out for
help, he gazes at the envelope containing Yvonne's third letter to him. As
he does, the reader cannot help but recall the contents of her second letter, in
which she wrote:

> Je ne m'inquiète pas trop de l'écrivain. En sacrifiant sa vie—celle des
> autres parfois—à la passion d'écrire, il suit peut-être, à tâtons, la voie
> que Dieu lui a tracée. . . . Non, vous n'êtes pas seul! Vous ne vivez
> pas seul: car un Autre vous accompagne. Et je vous dis que vous ne
> mourrez pas seul: Dieu n'oublie rien. (262)

With his eyes still fixed on the envelope, he says to himself: "Il y a quelque
chose pour moi, dans la lettre d'Yvonne Lebrun" (282). Then as his last
breath passes from his body, the novel's narrative voice tells us: "Il entra
dans un silence qui n'était pas le vide, et sa main sur le drap s'acharnait à
son dernier travail. Elle faisait le geste d'écrire" (282).

One cannot help but recall the denouement of Mauriac's *Nœud de
vipères* (1931) in which Louis seems to re-evaluate a lifetime of selfishness
and undergo the experience of conversion before he dies in the act of
writing. Like Mauriac, Saint Pierre is attempting to suggest the workings of
grace in Damville's soul. Through Yvonne's letters, the reader is left to
guess at the details of this experience, which is obviously not spelled out.
Like the three meetings that Louis had with the abbé de Calèse just before
his death, these three letters indicate in an indirect manner what might have
taken place in Damville's soul. Just as Mauriac cleverly offers no formal
and irrefutable evidence of Louis's conversion in *Nœud de vipères,* Saint
Pierre uses the same strategy here. Thus, while whoever discovered Alexandre lying dead in bed the next morning would have no reason to attach
any supernatural significance to an unopened letter from one of Damville's
admirers, the reader of the novel, who is aware of the contents of Yvonne
Lebrun's earlier letters, does recognize this possible dimension in the
envelope.

Saint Pierre's interest in the literary career of his distant cousin,
Henri de Montherlant, is apparent despite the author's explicit and
somewhat overstated disclaimer. Alexandre Damville not only espouses the
same general philosophy of life as did Montherlant (who, ironically,

committed suicide in 1972 at the age of 77), he even looks like him. For like Montherlant, he is "grand, mince de taille et large d'épaules" with "cheveux gris, coupés en brosse," all of which gives an observer the impression of "austérité athlétique" (20). Also, in naming the novel *Les Ecrivains,* Saint Pierre obviously wanted it to be associated with so many of Montherlant's novels with similar sounding titles, like *Les Olympiques* (1924), *Les Bestiaires* (1926), *Les Célibataires* (1934), and *Les Jeunes Filles* (1936). In addition, the title of *Les Ecrivains* was intended to exploit any residual success that might have come from the fact that the public would be able to identify the work easily with his own *Les Aristocrates* of several years earlier. In this case, however, the title was, and is, misleading and inappropriate. Although a generic, collective noun was entirely justified for *Les Aristocrates,* since the Marquis de Maubrun and his country *château* were clearly paradigmatic of a whole caste and its world view, *Les Ecrivains* does not deal with writers in general or with the politico-socio-literary intrigues of Latin Quarter publishing houses, but with one writer— and a somewhat eccentric one at that. A more appropriate and honest title might have been *Un Homme de lettres* or, as Emile Henriot suggested, *Le Glorieux,* but not *Les Ecrivains,* which seems intended to exploit association with both *Les Aristocrates* and Montherlant's novels.

Critical reaction to this novel was almost universally negative. Emile Henriot was probably the most acerbic. After giving his reader a résumé of the plot he asked: "Où est la littérature dans tout cela?" He goes on: "aucun écrivain digne de ce temps ne se reconnaîtra dans les personnages fausse-ment représentatifs du livre de Michel de Saint Pierre. La littérature, le souci des lettres, c'est ailleurs et c'est autre chose."[13]

Pierre de Boisdeffre was hardly more positive. Although con-ceding that the principal character was a powerful creation and recognizing once again "le talent, la vie jaillissante et les bonheurs d'écriture de l'auteur de *La Mer à boire,*" he was disappointed in the rest of the novel, including the misleading title and the fact that "les personnages secondaires ne sont que des esquisses."[14]

While I can understand these objections and share them to a certain degree, *Les Ecrivains* remains a significant work in Saint Pierre's *œuvre* because of what he was attempting to do in it. In so far as it reveals once again the author's attempt to use specifically Catholic material in his novel, including the reworking and adapting of insights of a significant predecessor like Mauriac, it enables us to situate him as a writer who at this point in his career was conscious of developing his vocation as a Catholic writer. In this regard, it prefigures his next novel, *Les Murmures de Satan,* which would be devoted to an analysis of the nature of Catholic spiritual life in a modern-style communal setting.

4. The Blossoming of a Catholic Novelist

LES NOUVELLES LITTÉRAIRES PUBLISHED *LES MURMURES DE SATAN* in weekly installments during the spring of 1959 before its release in book form. The fact that the novel was serialized in such a widely read and yet serious literary weekly testifies to Saint Pierre's growing prestige at this time. When asked by Gabriel d'Aubarède about the meaning of the book, Saint Pierre characterized it as his first truly Catholic novel: *"Les Murmures de Satan,* c'est aussi mon premier roman religieux. Et je l'ai voulu aussi orthodoxe que possible," he said. When asked if his main concern was to present the life of an experimental Christian community, he answered: "Non, C'en est le décor. Le véritable sujet, c'est le combat du bien et du mal, traité sous le biais de la tentation."[1] Calling *Les Aristocrates* "un tableau de mœurs," and *Les Ecrivains* "un tableau de caractères," he described *Les Murmures de Satan* both as an attempt to do something new as a novelist and to write from his own personal Christian point of view. This departure from his previous work was obvious. To Jean Blanzat, it was apparent that Saint Pierre was striving to rework subject matter dear to Bernanos. He wrote:

> Dans son cinquième roman Michel de Saint Pierre montre un souci de renouvellement et une ambition dont, dès l'abord, on lui sait gré. Il quitte les peintures balzaciennes des *Aristocrates* ou des *Ecrivains.* Dans un "roman catholique, et qui se veut tel," il s'attaque lui-même aux thèmes de Bernanos: la sainteté, la tentation.[2]

At the center of the novel is Satan, who is presented through the action of one of the characters. As for the "murmurs" of the title, Saint Pierre chose this word to indicate what in his opinion is Satan's ability to adapt to new conditions, his cleverness at attacking the unsuspecting, and his skill at encouraging them to mask their selfish and destructive actions in more altruistic and positive terms.

The hero and central figure of the novel is Jean Dewinter. He is a successful engineer, forty-two years of age, and the proprietor of his own electronics firm. He is a believing Christian who has already succeeded in bringing together three other married couples and three single people to live in a community. His view of Christianity is modern and forward-looking, and in this it resembles his esthetic tastes.

Writing on the eve of the announcement and convocation of the Second Vatican Council, which was going to transform dramatically the way in which Catholics look upon and interact with the modern world, Saint Pierre created a hero who is still credible today. In fact, this "prophetic" element in the book is quite striking at a distance of more than three decades, and a contemporary reader would have little difficulty imagining the action of the novel taking place in our day. Thus, when we recall that the novel was written in the mid-fifties and published in 1959, its continuing relevance to contemporary life is all the more astonishing.

Dewinter, as the modern practicing Catholic, is not afraid of the world of science, for through his university studies he has raised himself up from humble beginnings as the son of a factory worker in the northern city of Amiens, in French Flanders, to a position as owner of his own firm and husband of a daughter of the French aristocracy. Jean's wife, Monique, is the character in this novel who seems closest to the author's heart. She shares a reciprocal love for her husband and their five children, whose ages range from early infancy through adolescence. Married for fifteen years despite the initial opposition of Monique's parents, they have evolved together and deepened their relationship. Only the unusual circumstances of the Occupation permitted their courtship in the first place. Since 1945, they have managed not only to build a common life together, but have also brought together ten other people to share their existence in an eighteenth-century château that they rent in a Paris suburb.

The three other couples with whom they live include Geneviève Masson and her husband Robert. Geneviève's thirst for attention from men other than her husband is matched only by Robert's inability to see what she is doing. The second couple consists of Caroline Damiens and her husband Jacques, who has spent so much time reading the Bible and learned commentaries on it that he is afraid that he is about to lose his faith. Then there are the Saint-Benoists, whose first names we never learn. They are both biologists and have a son, Yves, whom they sacrifice to their work. The three single people are Christophe Souril, a student at the prestigious Ecole Normale Supérieure, Nicole Dumaine, a lesbian who is in love with Caroline Damiens, and, finally, Léo, a sculptor who resides in a remodeled greenhouse adjacent to the château.

As the novel opens, it is the beginning of June and all the actors are in place. The community has been functioning for a year already with the provisional approval of church authorities. At present, its future does not seem threatened, but by the end of the summer it will be ordered to disband. The abbé Muire, who has served as chaplain to the group since its creation, announces the news of the dissolution of the community at the end of the novel. Although no specific reason is given and no blame is placed on anyone, the reader finds it difficult not to agree that the community ought to be disbanded. Thus, on one level, the novel tells the story of the forces at work within and among the various members of the community and leads us from the heady idealism of shared Christian community life at the outset to the sobering conclusion that such utopian visions are most difficult, if not impossible, to realize without imposing the strictest laws to govern the conduct of community members.

On another level, the novel probes the inner workings of Jean Dewinter's mind. "Jean reste un sensuel, un orgueilleux emporté par l'action et qui ne prend pas assez le temps de méditer" (380), is the judgment made by the abbé Muire. Two special relationships preoccupy Jean: the one with Léo, the sculptor whom he is attempting to convert to Catholicism, and the one with his wife who, despite her longing to have an apartment or house of her own, tolerates her husband's desire to experiment with this new type of Christian life. In the end, her love for Jean causes her to want to share his hope that this pilot community will lead to the creation of other, similar efforts.

The community operates as such in three principal ways. The members take the evening meal together, devote one evening a week to the discussion of a religious topic, and share living expenses. Jean Dewinter sits at the head of the dinner table and presides over the weekly meetings, while Monique has been charged with the responsibility of keeping the books, a time-consuming and thankless task. Unfortunately, the novel never depicts the members of the community at one of their weekly meetings.

Regarding the community's three operating principles, one might be tempted to ask at the outset why they have not gone further. However, as the abbé Muire puts it, this is "une sorte de test exceptionnel, provisoire" (37), and prudence is called for. On the other hand, the four adult women and five adult men do, in fact, live in very close proximity, a situation that gives rise to special and often unexpected temptations, and often exerts a negative effect on the children. Thus, in a sense, they have already gone too far.

We never learn Léo's last name, but it is clear from the beginning that it is he who represents the forces of evil in the world. Jean, who admires his work as an artist, has personally recruited him as a member and, to house him suitably, has transformed the venerable old eighteenth-century "orangerie," or greenhouse, into an apartment/studio for the resident artist. He hopes to convert Léo, but it is the latter who never seems to pass up an opportunity to mock and insult both the community as a whole and its individual members, including Jean.

One cannot help but link Léo with the Satan of the novel's title. One of the epigrams that introduces the novel is the famous quote from Baudelaire: "la plus belle ruse du démon, c'est de nous persuader qu'il n'existe pas." And since one cannot in our skeptical age introduce Satan into the action of a work of art the way that Milton, in *Paradise Lost,* or Goethe, in *Faust,* were able to do in previous centuries, an intermediary, an earthly embodiment, is necessary. This role is assigned to Léo.

Saint Pierre took a serious risk in writing a novel about a Catholic lay person whom others, like the abbé Muire and most of the members of the community, consider to be a saint. At this point in his career he had already written the biography of Bernadette of Lourdes, and, a few years later, he would publish a biography of the curé of Ars. The subject of sainthood seems to have captured Saint Pierre's imagination at the time, even though he knew as well as anyone else that official canonization of lay persons has largely ceased in modern times, since the age of martyrs has passed. Nowadays, despite the many changes brought by Vatican II, it is still usually people who live a formal religious life (priests, brothers, nuns) who tend to be officially declared saints. And yet the day to day experience of many people testifies to the fact that there are indeed lay saints who stand out among other people despite their lack of formal religious vows. This underlying sense of recognition on the part of the reader enters into Saint Pierre's strategy in writing this novel: the widely held conviction that it is possible to be married, to live "in the world," and still be a saint.

The struggle in Jean's life between Monique on the one hand and Léo on the other is intensified as the novel builds to its climax. When Jean is able to have a new invention patented and then sells it to a larger firm, he is assured of an initial profit of 50 million old francs (i.e., about $100,000 in 1959 dollars). When he tells Monique of his excitement at this prospect because it will enable him to support the foundation of other communities modeled on his own, she is incredulous. Already upset by the potential "promiscuité" that haunts the members of the community, she sees this money as an opportunity for the family to buy their own apartment and adopt a more traditional lifestyle. She also thinks that money should be set aside for the children. But to Jean this laudable intent is still a lesser good than what he considers to be the Christian's obligation to share the misery and solitude of others.

Monique at this point accuses him of being unreasonable and reveals that she has already discovered that he has given away family possessions of material and sentimental value to various people almost on a whim—a gold piece inherited from his father, his silver watch, even the jade snuff box that she had given him as an engagement present. When confronted in this way, Jean is speechless. Defenseless, and feeling that his back is to the wall, he simply walks away from his wife.

This conversation, including its mute ending, serves to crystalize for the reader the age-old question of the Christian attitude toward money and wealth. How much is "enough"? Who is the "neighbor" that one must love and to whom one must give without question? Since Jean gives the narrowest possible answer to the first question and considers "enough" to be sufficient income to insure little more than family subsistence, while at the same time giving the widest possible answer to the second question, his immediate family does not automatically have any overwhelming claim, at least in theory, on him or his financial resources.

Léo, the sculptor, confronts Jean principally through the catalytic powers of a character named Rosaline. She is a nineteen-year-old who poses nude for Léo. She is still a virgin and has so far resisted Léo's advances. But once she meets Jean, she makes it clear that she will be his for the asking. She is therefore a potential source of conflict, especially since Léo has been insulting Jean for his religious idealism from the beginning of the novel. He systematically comes late to dinner and lets the members of the community know that he believes them to be fools. As Jean puts it, "Léo prétend que mes sentiments sont troubles, que je perds mon temps et que je suis indigne d'être un fondateur" (208). Why, we are tempted to ask, does Jean tolerate such a dissenter and troublemaker in their midst? Add to this the fact that Léo is attempting to seduce Geneviève Masson and at one point will even arouse the curiosity of Monique to such an extent that she comes to the greenhouse to see what he is working on, and the reader must conclude not only that Léo is an unlikely candidate for conversion, but also that he potentially threatens to destroy the whole experimental community. But this is how Saint Pierre must have it if he is to introduce a figure around whom all the evil in the novel must converge.

In the greenhouse, Léo works sporadically on the bust of a figure that he keeps draped most of the time. Later, when the situation has reached the breaking point and Jean finally goes to tell Léo that he will have to leave, the latter confesses that each time that he works on this project it gets away from him to such an extent that he invariably finds himself sculpting his own image, and not that of Christ which he had originally intended to do. Touched by this confession, Jean has a change of heart, but even while doing so he notices the hint of what looks like a satanical grin pass across Léo's face:

> Non pas un sourire, qui laisse au coin des lèvres un peu de mystère et de beauté, mais bien un rire, bref et silencieux. Son visage en devenait vulgaire—car le rire détruit ce qu'il touche. Léo rassembla dans ses traits, une seconde, l'âpre ironie du mensonge et le mépris du dupeur triomphant. (266)

Jean has been face to face with Satan.

Clearly, the struggle between Jean and Léo is an avatar of the battle between good and evil that structures the whole novel. This conclusion is reinforced when we learn that Léo might even be "possessed" (289). But Jean, who looks up the textbook definition of diabolical possession in the *Rituel Romain*, is not deterred. Léo's conduct might very well be satanical and he might also be possessed by the devil, but to Jean the only thing that counts is to extend the hand of Christian love to Léo. Although the abbé Muire has warned him that he is running a senseless risk in allowing Léo to stay on, he still feels compelled to do so.

But is this not the courage that true and genuine saints are supposed to have? Should they not be able to meet Satan face to face and to risk doing battle with him on his own terms? To these questions we can answer both yes and no. Yes, because there can be no doubt that the lives of the saints are replete with dramatic and often personally incarnated confrontations with evil. No, in the sense that these confrontations are usually if not always such that it is the devil who seeks out the potential saint and not the other way around. Here, on the contrary, it is Jean who brings into his life an eminently evil, selfish, and destructive person on the pretext that he wants to convert him. In this sense, despite what others might think of him, Jean is really not following in the footsteps of the saints. In fact, his principal motivation, if anything, seems to be pride.

The Bernanosian dimension in the novel is apparent, for the confrontation with Léo, a Satan figure, is reminiscent of the nocturnal meeting between the diabolical horse trader and the abbé Donissan in *Sous le soleil de Satan*. But at the same time there is a sense of humor in Saint Pierre's work that is generally absent in Bernanos. As the critic Henriette Charasson points out about Saint Pierre, "l'auteur sait mêler la distinction et la familiarité, le tragique avec la drôlerie."[3] In fact, she might have gone a step further and indicated that the structural counterpoint that she hints at here is at the very heart of the novel. Flagrant oppositions of all kinds abound in the work and Saint Pierre as novelist seems to be attempting to search for some middle ground amidst all the contrasts and contradictions.

In addition to the opposition between the ideal of Christian poverty and the practical necessity of money that Jean (a self-made man) and Monique (a born aristocrat) must face, there is also, as mentioned above, the struggle between Jean (idealism and unreasonable generosity) and Léo (skepticism and inveterate selfishness). But there is also the stark contrast between the youthfulness, vivaciousness, and exuberance incarnated by Rosaline, Léo's model, and old age, death, and hopelessness as seen in Jean's employee, Gros Louis, who is slowly dying of cancer. In fact, toward the end of the novel, Jean counterbalances the seductive urgings of Rosaline by spending every available free minute at Gros Louis's bedside, doing all that he can to prepare him for death. The use of counterpoint in the novel was especially striking to Lucien Guissard: "Il pose le problème de l'apostolat d'un laïc qui a des responsabilités familiales; il oppose l'apostolat et le devoir d'état, la charité et le devoir de prévoyance, le péché et la grâce, l'audace et la prudence."[4]

Another striking contrast exists between the lay people who see themselves as pioneers blazing a trail for other Christians to follow and the abbé Muire, their chaplain, who preaches caution, prudence, and moderation. Due to an article that he had previously published describing the life of the community, he has received some twenty inquiries from other people interested in founding communities of their own. This enthusiastic reaction only serves to underscore his cautious feelings about the community, and when he decides not to respond to the letters it is only because his misgivings are already so strong. There are simply too many risks involved. With the adults living together under the same roof, there is inevitably what he calls the "promiscuité de chaque instant" (72). He adds to this, however, that the children are confused by not living in a traditional family unit—and this risk of scandal might in the long run be the gravest danger of all. "Pour protéger les âmes," he says, "il faut savoir renoncer à la joie de prendre des risques" (76). The members of the community, with the sole exception of Monique, however, are committed to making the community a success. They have no doubts or hesitation. To them the twentieth century is the age of the group, as reflected in the widespread existence and general acceptance of labor unions, professional associations, political parties, special interest groups of all kinds, and even gangs. Thus, as products of their age, they want to live together in an attempt to give a human face to the practice of charity. This conflict, one can even call it antagonism, between lay persons and their clerical leader, permeates the whole novel and is, once again, also a prophetic theme, for it announces the discord that would come to the fore so often in the life of the church during the sixties and beyond, with individual lay persons and groups often galloping ahead of the slower moving institutional church and its hierarchy.

The community's experiment has gone about as far as it can go and has tested the limits of orthodoxy, but here again the novel is prophetic of the actions of those thousands of Catholics in the industrialized nations of the world who have engaged in experimental ways of living over the past twenty years even though their experiments have not been approved by Rome. When reprimanded, rather than leave the church and create a new one of their own, they have simply continued on their way and paid little or no attention to hierarchical disapproval. In this regard, Saint Pierre has his finger on one of the key aspects of our age: the desire to change the church from within, to rethink the ancient commission given to the apostles and express it in terms fit for the present age, but within the limits and boundaries of orthodoxy. The community in this novel, like the church itself, is thus bulging with centrifugal forces and energies that in another age would have given rise to the creation of splinter groups and factions, each one listening to its own music. These forces are contained, however, by the centripetal force at work—a power that inspires a certain respect for traditions and reminds the adventuresome of the ultimate futility or creating yet another group in the name of Christ.

The novel closes on a final note that is both ironic and optimistic. After receiving the news that the community must disband, Jean hastens to the bedside of Gros Louis, a widower, to be with him as he lies dying. But since the man's teenage son, who is somewhat of a juvenile delinquent, will also soon be an orphan, Jean's immediate reaction is to offer to take the boy into his own home as a foster child. But here he hesitates, for he knows how happy Monique is to have the community finally disbanded. She now looks forward to a change of living quarters and a more traditional "bourgeois" way of life. But as Jean finally gets home from the hospital in the middle of the night and crawls into bed, Monique whispers to him: "J'ai réfléchi à ce gosse, au fils de ton ouvrier: tu ne crois pas qu'il faut le prendre avec nous?" (288). Monique, who had seemed closed to the possibility of further risk-taking, is in fact still quite open. A middle way between the excess of the community's experiment and the refusal to do anything to aid one's neighbor is within reach. Thus, Christian charity as practiced within the framework of the traditional family unit seems to be the route that Jean and Monique will follow. In this way they avoid the extreme of doing nothing for the boy. But at the other extreme there can no longer be any question of raising him in the community—an alternative that almost surely would not have worked to his benefit.

Pierre Grenaud seems to have been the first critic to have used the term "témoin de son temps"[5] in speaking of Michel de Saint Pierre's novels. The term is correct in that the first four novels were each clearly based either on a social milieu with which he was familiar or on his own personal experience. But here, writing for the first time as an historian or chronicler of contemporary society, he breaks new ground. Thus, the novel takes a double risk, both in its subject matter as a "roman catholique" and in the relationship of that subject matter to Saint Pierre's earlier work.

A useful comparison can be made between *Les Murmures de Satan* and Gilbert Cesbron's *Les Saints vont en enfer* (1952) in that they both deal with an experiment in Christian community living. But whereas Cesbron treated in his novel the efforts of priests to share the living conditions of de-Christianized working class people in the late forties and early fifties, Saint Pierre offers a portrait of convinced Christians from a bourgeois background. A further difference is that Cesbron clearly supports the experiment that he depicts, even though his readers know that the movement has been discontinued on orders from Rome. Here, however, unlike Cesbron, Saint Pierre turns out to be unsympathetic to the experiment that he describes, although we only come to this conclusion gradually, especially toward the end of the novel. He deeply appreciates and respects the generosity and good will of the community's founder and lay leader, Jean Dewinter, but these qualities alone prove insufficient to assure the spiritual success of the community.

As mentioned above, Saint Pierre was aware in writing *Les Murmures de Satan* that he was moving from what was primarily a *tableau de mœurs* to a *roman religieux* or *roman catholique*. It is significant, however, that he places prime emphasis on the personal and social connections between people attempting to create a Christian community, rather than concentrate on deep psychological analysis of his characters. As a result, the reader has the impression of watching a film, for we get to know the characters primarily from the outside, from what they say and do and not because of a heavy-handed authorial intervention in their inner life. In this respect, Saint Pierre was clearly striving to give fresh impetus to the Catholic novel in his day. This fact was noted by André Billy who wrote: "Je le trouve ici en très net progrès sur les ouvrages qui ont assuré sa jeune gloire. Il s'est, dans *Les Murmures de Satan,* attaqué à un sujet dont la hauteur fait honneur à ses ambitions."[6] In the final analysis, this novel of a spiritual failure is itself a successful work of art that Paul Guth has summed up as follows: "Sur un fond de réalisme rassurant, Michel de Saint Pierre a su donner à sa fable la grandeur et le mystère qui rejoignent les légendes éternelles des forces de la nature."[7]

The fictional Collège Pierre-Favre is located just outside the city of Paris in one of its more affluent suburbs. As in all Jesuit secondary schools, the most powerful and important positions are held by the *préfet de discipline,* in this case le père Raphael Menuzzi, and the Principal, or *recteur,* le père Dalival. Menuzzi has received from the students the nickname "La Tigresse" because of his stealth in prowling throughout the school. *Le père recteur,* Dalival, on the other hand, is generally considered by students and teachers alike to be a kind of saint. He is detached from the ways of the world, while being consistently open to and fair with students.

Before writing *Les Nouveaux Aristocrates,* Saint Pierre employed his customary Balzacian strategy by returning to his old secondary school, Saint-Jean-de-Béthune in Versailles, where he sat in on classes and lived in close proximity to students and faculty for several weeks. Although the city of Versailles is never mentioned in the novel, the fictional Collège Pierre-Favre is in the Seine-et-Oise department, whose administrative center at the time was Versailles.

As individual schools do not grant the *baccalauréat* diploma on their own authority in France, this privilege being reserved to the state, the national examinations administered each June take on enormous importance. In 1960, when the action of this novel takes place, the pre-1968 system, considerably more selective than the present one, still prevailed. At the time, only about 40 percent of the candidates for the *bac* passed the combined written and oral exam on the first attempt. Against this tense and competitive background, Saint Pierre focuses our attention, during the crucial months of April and May, on a group of students preparing for the exam in their final year of secondary school, *la classe de philosophie.* They have suddenly been deprived of their beloved teacher, the philosopher Alfred Sauvageot, victim of a heart attack. On short notice, le père de Maubrun, the Marquis's son from *Les Aristocrates,* has been summoned to the school and assigned as Sauvageot's replacement. His uncertainty about his own aptitude for teaching a class on this level is then exacerbated when he finds himself in conflict with one of the students, Denis Prullé-Rousseau, who exercises a preponderant influence on his classmates.

Maubrun has only been recently ordained and had requested to be sent abroad somewhere as a missionary. Instead, not only has he been retained in France, he has also been sent to teach this secondary school class even though he is considered to be a rising theologian with several learned articles to his credit. The only previous experience that he has had on this level is a year of teaching religion to fourteen-year-olds (*classe de 5e*) in the famous Jesuit institution, the Collège Franklin, several years earlier. Thus, despite his vow of obedience, he feels ill-equipped late in the school year to step into a classroom and replace a master teacher like Alfred Sauvageot, whose sense of discipline was somewhat relaxed by Jesuit standards, and whose liberal and excessively tolerant attitudes about student conduct had endeared him to his class. Just as le père de Maubrun is urged by his superior to go into the class in order to bring the group back under control and prepare them for their *bac*, so also the students, inspired by Denis, have vowed to sabotage his efforts.

As in *La Mer à boire*, where at the beginning of the novel Saint Pierre presents to us the Van Hussel family gathered around the dinner table in a moment of crisis for the rebellious young man of the family, we also first get to know Denis Prullé-Rousseau and his family at an elaborate luncheon at his home. His parents have invited maître Martincourt, the celebrated lawyer, and Eloi Delisnière, the well-known writer of "œuvres précieuses et difficiles qu'il appelait *Suites poétiques*—et dont les femmes du monde se raffolaient sans en comprendre un mot" (36). Denis deliberately arrives late. His long-suffering mother would like to give her seventeen year old son a good scolding, but contents herself, in front of her guests, with a dirty look. His father, in the tradition of the *grand bourgeois* presiding over his table, does not even seem to be aware of his son's presence. The discussion touches upon the important topics of the day: the agonizing death throes of the Fourth Republic, the war in Algeria, the meaning of modern art, and the question of capital punishment. As Denis sees things, there are profound disagreements among the people at the table on each issue, but nonetheless each man is careful to mask his true opinion in order to be conciliatory. Bourgeois privilege is maintained, he surmises, by remaining discreet and not causing turmoil. "Leur règle du jeu est de ne pas se compromettre, de se ménager entre amis, de bouffer le canard en paix et d'avancer dans leur petit boulot" (39), he says to himself as he witnesses their conversation. True to the code, his father is the most inscrutable of all, for Denis has no idea what he thinks about the important questions in life. At the same time, he must admit that the forty-five year old is both handsome and elegant. Although an authority figure, he is not truly an "adult" to Denis because he is not really "old." Finally, as coffee and brandy are brought to the table by their Senegalese manservant, his father asks him what is new at school. In response, Denis attacks le père de Maubrun and denounces the school authorities for planning to send into their class a young, inexperienced teacher who would have preferred to be a missionary. But his father is not listening. Instead, we see him now playing the role of father by tapping on his wristwatch as a sign that it is time for Denis to get back to school. The boy leaves the house without saying a word to anyone, jumps on his scooter and returns to school for his afternoon classes.

Before we see Maubrun locked in battle with his class, we learn that he has already asked Dalival for a change of assignment. In refusing this request, the Principal reminds him that in this particular case, as in so many others, humility requires that he accept a decision made by his superiors. Furthermore, says Dalival, since so many parents have abdicated their responsibility toward their children, he will be just as real and authentic a missionary here as he would have been if he had been sent to Africa.

Maubrun tries to ingratiate himself with his new class upon their first meeting by speaking warmly of Sauvageot and reading to them from some little-known texts written by their former teacher. Nonetheless, they are hostile to him and easily let him know that he is already a failure as a teacher. They want him to give up right away. During the next few days, as Maubrun patiently strives to communicate, he becomes more successful. But each success only increases Denis's alienation and resentment. After about a week has gone by, we hear Maubrun telling the class that society is headed toward the creation of a world without real culture, because the humanities are under attack on all sides. Everything, he claims prophetically, is being sacrificed to the teaching either of science or of pre-professional and vocational skills. Young people are no longer being taught to think, to write and to express themselves. The students seem very interested and we soon find them hanging on every word—all except Denis. As an act of aggression, he remains seated in the back of the class reading his *cahier vert*, the green notebook in which he had taken his notes during Sauvageot's lectures. Maubrun, finally provoked to wrath, calmly walks by Denis's seat and, lifting him up with one hand, tears the notebook from his hand with the other. Just at that moment, Menuzzi, "la Tigresse," comes into the classroom with the results of the "petit bac" exam, a preparation test for the formal *baccalauréat* scheduled for June. Both Maubrun and the class conceal from him what has just taken place and listen attentively as he announces that the top grade in the class belongs to Denis Prullé-Rousseau.

Denis, after having had his green notebook taken from him at the end of morning classes, decides not to go home for lunch. Instead, he goes to a little *café* a few blocks from school called *The Three Stars*, which is frequented by people who steal merchandise from an unnamed American military installation located nearby. Inevitably, the reader realizes that we have here the fictional transformation of the U.S. SHAPE headquarters, located in Versailles until the mid-sixties when France formally withdrew from NATO. Coming here, Denis plunges himself into another social milieu, one that is quite different from his own. Feeling pressured in school and ignored at home, he is seeking escape.

After lunch, he decides not to return to school for the afternoon session, and it is about this time that several American soldiers arrive. They are selling records, whiskey, and cigarettes stolen from the American PX. Despite their civilian attire, he can still recognize them from afar as Americans since they always seem to be chomping on chewing gum. Soon youngsters from a local *lycée* come in. They are wearing American style jeans and go right to the jukebox to listen to American rock records. Here, the sordid world without culture is associated with Americans and their way of life. We are reminded of Barbara Lee, the American fiancée of Rémy Belfontaine in *La Mer à boire*. Her willingness to make love to Marc van Hussel in Rémy's absence is partially explained by the fact that she is an American.

It is already evening when Denis finally leaves *The Three Stars* café. Instead of returning home, he goes to visit M. Thibéron, the printer of the monthly review that Denis and his classmates have recently begun to publish. Called *Le Meneur*, it already has several subscribers, but of course continues to lose money. Thibéron, so far, has not forced him to settle accounts. He is in no hurry to collect money that is owed to him if it means killing *Le Meneur*. Denis's next stop is at an antique shop where he buys an old Russian icon for his friend, an eighty-two year old Russian emigré whom he knows only by the name of "Le Colonel" and whom he had met in the shop by chance six months earlier. To Denis, the colonel represents wisdom and serenity and he replaces Sauvageot as an adult whom he can admire. He spends almost all of his money on the icon and asks that the shop owner deliver it as a present and not reveal where it came from in order not to embarrass the colonel. Then, leaving the store, he stops a passing bum and gives him the remaining money in his pocket. As this transaction takes place, the reader realizes that the colonel counterbalances the Americans represented by the café that Denis has just come from and that he is a symbol of that other foreign influence that haunts French youth: atheistic Communism. As a refugee from the satanical deeds carried out in the name of Marxist ideology, the colonel seems to represent all that is pure in Russian culture (we recall Saint Pierre's intimate knowledge of modern Russian history as mirrored in his detailed two-volume history of the Romanovs), and which in turn has been suppressed and exiled by the triumphant Communists.

This chapter is the turning point of the novel, for it focuses on *Le Meneur*, whose continued publication will eventually cause Denis's expulsion from school. At the same time, it shows us that he is not nearly as bad a person as he would like to think he is, for he anonymously buys a present for someone and then gives away to a stranger what is left of his money.

Finally returning home, Denis learns that his mother has gone to a dinner at the home of Delisnière, while his father has not come home yet. His eighteen year old sister, Marie-Bénédicte, discusses with him the breakdown in the relationship between their parents. She knows, for instance, that their father has had a succession of lovers and they discover in going through their father's appointment calendar, that he is planning to attend a professional meeting in Rome with the latest of them, Danielle Manourgias. To Denis, this comes as no shock, but his sister, Marie-Bénédicte, is outraged. After Denis goes to bed, their mother also comes in and goes to bed without asking where her husband might be, but Marie-Bénédicte vows to wait up for her father and to create a scene about his mistresses when he returns. The attempt at communication is aborted because when Doctor Prullé-Rousseau returns, he has just left the operating room where he has been at work trying to save the life of eight year old Liliane. But since Liliane has just died despite his best efforts, the man is depressed as well as fatigued. Marie-Bénédicte, seeing her father in this state, prefers to say nothing. Another opportunity for communication between the generations has been lost.

This scene, in which words of reproach are prepared by the daughter but never uttered, reminds us that this novel is also about the problems of communication in modern life. As with the words of Sauvageot that Denis had carefully copied down in his *cahier vert*, he only reads and heeds the words that coincide with his intentions of the moment. The master's thoughts on human freedom are taken to heart, but his teachings about personal responsibility and religious faith are systematically ignored.

When Denis returns to school the next day, his absence and disruptive behavior will have enabled Menuzzi to convince Dalival that Denis ought to be expelled unless publication of *Le Meneur* ceases immediately. In the meantime, Maubrun thumbs through the *cahier vert* until he finds a letter from Professor Sauvageot to Denis: "Mon Cher Denis," it reads, "Je vous remercie de votre lettre. Mais vous vous plaignez trop. N'attendez pas de moi que je vous plaigne à mon tour. Vous avez la chance de vivre. . ." (156). At this point, Maubrun discreetly closes the notebook, for he realizes that to continue to read would be a serious invasion of the boy's privacy. Gradually, he is becoming Denis's spiritual father. As such, he feels the need to respect his spiritual son.

When Denis comes to retrieve his notebook, Maubrun asks him why he is behaving as he is—in fact deliberately provoking the event that had taken place the day before. "Parce que vous êtes un curé" (159), he responds. But then when asked what he is doing in a Catholic school if he does not like priests, he retorts: "Je ne crois pas en Dieu. Je n'aime pas les prêtres. Je n'ai pas demandé à être élevé ici, dans une boîte de Jèzes. Mais vous voyez, c'est drôle: je tiens à rester au collège. Je tiens à y faire mes Maths-Elems l'année prochaine. J'y suis chez moi. Et d'ailleurs. . ." (160). Untouched by grace and without faith, Denis has no place else to go. Even as a disruptive student, he has more of an identity here than anywhere else.

Until now, le père de Maubrun has been thinking on and off about the parable of the Good Shepherd who temporarily abandons the ninety-nine sheep who are safely in the fold to seek out the one that has gone astray. This must be the only reason, the reader is tempted to tell himself, why Maubrun continues to take so much abuse from this boy. But when we recall other Saint Pierre creations, like Jean Dewinter in *Les Murmures de Satan*, who tolerates the presence of the atheist Léo in his experimental Christian community even though the latter is evidently attempting to sabotage all that Jean is trying to accomplish, we realize that this theme is a constant in Saint Pierre's work: the necessity of direct confrontation with evil on the part of the person who seeks sanctity.

Finally, when it becomes clear that Denis intends to defy school authorities by publishing *Le Meneur* and, in so doing, continue to proclaim his avowed atheism to the rest of the school, le père de Maubrun arranges a visit with his father in the hope that the latter will be able to dissuade him from his planned course of action. But since Dr. Prullé-Rousseau is planning on leaving for Italy the next day and Mme Prullé-Rousseau is on vacation in England, neither one of them will have the time to discuss the matter with their son and thus another opportunity for communication will be lost. But in the course of the conversation between the Jesuit and Denis's father, Dr. Prullé-Rousseau agrees that he has lost control of his children and failed as a parent, but still wonders, almost naively, why they do not love and respect him anyway. As the priest leaves the father's apartment, he realizes that this chain of events will inexorably lead to Denis's dismissal from school. The die has been cast.

The following Monday the latest edition of *Le Meneur* is clandestinely distributed in school. Dalival has Maubrun bring Denis to his office right away. He wants to ask the boy if he is responsible for the following statement that defends his right to freedom of speech, despite the impact of his words within the context of the Catholic school community:

> Si je dis que vos liturgies et vos cérémonies sont désuètes, j'en ai le droit. Si je dis que les évangiles ne sont que des recettes d'hygiène morale et sociale, j'en ai le droit . . . Et si je dis que votre Christ était peut-être un sage—mais que le monde où je vis attend d'autres sages, et qu'il est grand temps qu'ils viennent—prétendez-vous m'en contester le droit? (142-43)

When Dalival asks Denis why he has written this, he answers that Professor Sauvageot had always assured him that he was first and foremost a free man and that human liberty comes before all else. Dalival calmly turns in his chair and, taking a copy of one of Sauvageot's books from the shelf, reads: "La liberté, qui est tout, n'est pas grand-chose hors des rigueurs de l'obéissance. Mais il faut, pour comprendre cela, une vie de prière, de réflexion, et d'amour" (244). Denis retorts that although Sauvageot was a believer, he did not impose his personal beliefs on his students and that le père de Maubrun should not do so now. To this Dalival responds that it is he alone and not the philosophy teacher who is expelling him from school and who takes complete responsibility for this action.

After packing up his belongings, Denis races home and bursts into his father's study where he knows that he can find enough barbiturates to commit suicide. He drops a number of capsules in a glass and, while waiting for them to dissolve, picks up the green notebook and reads for the last time the letter from Sauvageot, the one that le père de Maubrun had begun to read but not finished:

> N'ecoutez jamais ceux qui tendent à vous écarter de vous-même, à vous dégoûter de vous-même, car vous avez la grâce d'être unique devant Dieu, irremplaçable et libre . . . Et si je me croyais digne de vous laisser un message en m'en allant, je vous dirais, sans craindre

> d'évoquer l'Evangile, que vous avez d'abord un être à aimer, à
> compromettre, à défendre, à sauver et à donner: vous-même! (252-53)

Refreshed by this renewed contact with his master, he throws the glass containing the dissolved pills against the wall and falls on his bed in a fit of laughter.

In the meantime, le père de Maubrun begs his superior to reconsider and to take Denis back. He reads the passage about the lost sheep from the gospel of St. Matthew and asks for permission to go after the lost sheep of his class. But Dalival responds that the passage refers only to Christ himself and ought not to be applied rigorously to human situations. "Ma décision est prise," he tells Maubrun, "Je vous demande à présent d'y adhérer. Même si vous êtes dans la nuit. Et je désire que nous n'en parlions plus" (254). As the novel ends, Denis is alone, but alive, while Maubrun, now clearly his spiritual father, reluctantly conforms to the wishes of his superior.

One of the striking things about this novel is the successful recreation by Saint Pierre of daily life at the *collège*. We have only sketched above the main outline of the plot, but within the narrative mechanism he evokes with realism and sympathy the day to day highs and lows of the school community: the excitement of the learning (and teaching) process when a talented and dedicated teacher interacts with a class full of bright and gifted students; the pranks carried out by the two fourteen year old trouble-makers, Truchaud and Quentillard; the patient labor of le père Menuzzi to somehow catch them in the act; and the life of the Jesuit community itself, composed as it is of terribly different kinds of people of widely varying ages and backgrounds, but all united around Loyola's educational philosophy, the *ratio studiorum*. In addition to Dalival, Maubrun and Menuzzi, we also meet le père Spitzwald, who is fanatically devoted to classical French drama, as well as the Jesuit brothers (like the unforgettable gardener Marcel), who performs the necessary nonintellectual tasks at school.

The first key that can be used to unlock the significance of this work can be found in the "Avertissement" that precedes the novel. Here, as usual, Saint Pierre attempts to give his reader some idea of what he is up to. He begins:

> J'appelle nouveaux aristocrates les très jeunes héros de ce roman, parce
> qu'ils seront une part de l'élite à venir . . . L'élite n'est pas seulement

supérieure: elle est différente . . . Ces nouveaux aristocrates—quel que soit leur milieu social—se reconnaissent à des traits de raffinement, d'exigence et d'inquiétude. Ils veulent bien autre chose au monde qu'être heureux—ou, plus précisément, être heureux ne représente jamais pour eux le véritable but. (9)

There seem to be two central issues raised here: 1) the elite individual is not only superior to the rest of his contemporaries, he is also different, and 2) being happy in life is not his major concern. Regarding the first point, there is no great difficulty in granting that Saint Pierre is basically correct. The elite adolescents at a Jesuit college, mostly but not totally recruited among the upper and more established strata of French society, would differ from most of their contemporaries in a sample cross-section of the population because of their privileged background. Saint Pierre is reminding us that French society has always been dominated and led by a relatively small elite group which, to a large extent, whether of the traditional Catholic or free-thinking vein, tend to perpetuate themselves in positions of power from generation to generation. But if we recall René Le Steyr of *Ce Monde ancien*, we can see that this theme of the aristocratic individual had been one of Saint Pierre's preoccupations from the beginning of his career. Like the young men of the college Pierre-Favre, René is superior to his contemporaries despite the social handicap of his working class background. And like the elite young people who would precipitate the events of 1968 a few short years later, adolescents like Denis Prullé-Rousseau and René Le Steyr are not satisfied with outmoded answers to the questions that haunt their generation.

The problem of happiness, however, as Saint Pierre defines it, is an altogether different matter because it has caused confusion among readers. If by happiness he means material comfort, a sense of selfishness reinforced by class standing and a general disregard for others, then the new aristocrats are truly indifferent to happiness. They no longer wear the social blinders that characterized their forebears of earlier generations. This, however, does not seem to be the primary meaning that Saint Pierre sought to give to the term in the novel. He expresses this meaning only in more detail toward the end of the book in an exchange between Geoffroy de Laval and Maubrun during philosophy class: "Je ne pense jamais au bonheur," proclaims Geoffroy (183), and the priest approves of the statement because he himself often repeats to himself the words attributed to Mary during her apparition to Bernadette at Lourdes: "Je ne vous promets pas que vous serez heureux dans ce monde, mais dans l'autre" (184). Thus, the definition of happiness that is offered here is of a very special and uncommon variety, for it is unattainable in life. Most people, especially those who are unbelievers, would disagree with such a statement, for it seems self-evident that all human beings, consciously or unconsciously, are seeking their own form of personal happiness. Furthermore, human life and civilization have often been led to ruin by doctrines that propose that human happiness is a lesser good than strength or power exerted through imposition of one's will upon others. After all, Denis Prullé-Rousseau is a good illustration of this danger, because the word happiness means nothing to him. Instead he feels compelled through a higher sense of duty to impose his own will upon others by proclaiming his atheistic beliefs to his fellow students in a Catholic school environment. But Saint Pierre still tries to get the last word in, for he seems to agree with Maubrun who, after having discussed this subject at length with his students, declares: "Le bonheur n'est pas *de ce monde*; pas davantage que le Royaume. Mais il faut être un héros ou un saint pour s'en détacher sans orgueil" (185).

This is exactly the point that should be remembered with reference to Maubrun's fascination with the Virgin's words to Bernadette at Lourdes. These words are not intended for ordinary Christians and were addressed in this context to a future saint. It is important to recall that Saint Pierre's biography of Bernadette places a good deal of emphasis on this fact. From the moment she claimed to have witnessed her apparitions, through her life in the convent where she encountered small-mindedness and jealousy, to her early death, she never seems to have been really happy. The confusion arises unfortunately from Saint Pierre's seeming to apply to all the "new aristocrats" words that were intended only for a future saint.

Les Nouveaux Aristocrates was generally well received as a novel in which the author displayed once again his ability to break new ground and to deal with a different subject in a fresh way. Louis Chaigne's positive reaction was typical.

> Il vient une heure dans la vie d'un écrivain, où tout se coalise pour permettre à des ressources et à des dons . . . de s'harmoniser et de s'épanouir en une œuvre où il s'exprime tout entier. Cette heure-là semble être arrivée pour Michel de Saint Pierre. A quarante-quatre ans,

il avait déjà compté des réussites et des succès. *Les Nouveaux Aristocrates* me paraissent représenter un sensible dépassement. C'est un livre de poids en même temps qu'un message de lumière.[8]

Emile Henriot had a similar opinion:

Solides, sérieux, bien écrits, ces *Nouveaux Aristocrates* sont déjà un livre de grande qualité par l'élévation du débat, la franche rigueur du dialogue où chacun marquera ses points, les raisons reconnues à l'un et à l'autre, et l'essai tenté d'explication de ce fameux mal de la jeunesse.[9]

Critical interest was attracted to the theme of Maubrun as Denis's spiritual father, who replaces the inept biological father. While Marie-Bénédicte is capable of filling the emptiness in her life the way many of her contemporaries do—through an active social life, alcohol and sexual experimentation—Denis, as an emblem of the elite in his generation, cannot be contented with such trifles. Put there in the first place by his father for reasons of family tradition and social standing more than out of any real concern for his moral and religious training and well-being, Denis only comes to realize after his expulsion that his college was the one place where he did have a sense of belonging. "Je n'aimais au monde," he says to one of his friends, "que cette sale boîte de collège. On n'avait pas le droit de me vider" (249). Has Denis been banished from school because of failure to cooperate with grace made available to him? Or has grace been denied to him? Saint Pierre remains ambiguous on this point. Thus we are left with the problem of the Catholic school failing to evangelize its most brilliant student.

Saint Pierre's reputation as a Catholic novelist was reinforced by the great success of *Les Nouveaux Aristocrates*. He struck a sensitive chord in extolling the life of a Jesuit secondary school and sympathetically treating the faculty charged with the difficult task of communicating with adolescents whose parents can no longer reach them. To cite but two examples, Lucien Guissard called the novel a "hommage rendu au collège chrétien,"[10] while Jean Nicollier declared: "Voilà une pierre de plus au monument que les Lettres élèvent aujourd'hui aux jésuites."[11] Four years later, with the publication of *Les Nouveaux Prêtres*, Saint Pierre would become the most controversial Catholic writer of his generation in France—and maybe even the most important.

5. *Les Nouveaux Prêtres*

RENE-MARILL ALBERES WAS CORRECT WHEN HE NOTED THAT A GOOD part of the impact of *Les Nouveaux Prêtres*[1] can be explained by the fact that the novel exploded at a time when the literary vogue had shifted away from committed writing into more sterile and esoteric concerns, like the ones reflected in the *nouveau roman* of the day. "Michel de Saint Pierre," he wrote, "se fait et se veut écrivain 'engagé.' Voilà ce qui nous intéresse ici: depuis dix ans, on n'en voyait plus beaucoup d'écrivains engagés."[2]

Les Nouveaux Prêtres, which compares the traditional forms of French Catholicism with the new ones that were evolving, at that very moment, out of the Second Vatican Council (1962-65), aroused a great controversy, both pro and con, in France. It succeeded first of all in enraging France's left-leaning Catholics, including a good percentage of the hierarchy, by seeming to accuse them of succumbing to the temptation of modernism, of watering down dogma and traditional moral beliefs in order to be inoffensive to Marxists and other non-Catholics. In doing so, the novel also served as a rallying cry for those millions of French Catholics who felt that the church was steering too hard toward the left in its attempt to shed its image as the supporter of bourgeois rank and privilege. While many of these supporters were surely "intégristes" of the type who refused most of the changes coming from the Council, many were no doubt ordinary people who saw the novel as an attempt to expose abuses and to argue for the retention of traditional devotional practices. In short, the novel was read at the time primarily as a *roman à thèse,* and in the process its artistic merits were overlooked. Now, some twenty-five years later, it is apparent that what the novel seemed to point out as "abuses" have become common devotional practice. Both the church and the world in which it lives have changed dramatically. Thus, it is now possible to take a fresh look at the novel and see it for what it is: a work that is Saint Pierre's most prophetic novel at the same time that it is much more subtle than anyone gave it credit for being at the time.

While the novel might very well have been the most widely talked about piece of fiction of the sixties, all the books, articles, interviews, and TV and radio talk about it were impassioned and highly partisan. In addition, Saint Pierre did not help matters much by seeming to be content to have the book read as a simple *roman à thèse*. When he published two books, both journalistic works, on the heels of *Les Nouveaux Prêtres*, each one exploiting research he had done for the novel, he gave the impression that the novel was to be read as simply another polemical work and not a work of art. Thus, anyone today who reads *Ces Prêtres qui souffrent* (1966), a collection of letters and documents relating to the difficulties experienced by many, mostly older, priests in dealing with the new procedures of the sixties, or *Sainte Colère* (1965), a frankly hostile pamphlet against Vatican II, cannot help but conclude that these works, although interesting even today, reflect the passions and viewpoints of the day. *Les Nouveaux Prêtres*, however, has aged well and reflects the tensions inherent in the conflict between the old church and the new church better than any other work of fiction at the time or in the intervening quarter century.

The action of *Les Nouveaux Prêtres* is set in Villedieu, a fictional northern suburb of Paris located in the so-called "red belt" of industrial towns bordering on Paris between Courbevoie and Saint-Denis and known for their densely packed industrial plants and largely Communist-dominated municipal councils. The parish priests in this area face an overwhelmingly difficult problem due to the neglect shown by the church to the interests and needs of working class people since the industrial revolution seized France in the middle of the nineteenth century. There was no disagreement in France in the mid-sixties between "intégriste" and "progressiste" Catholics about the fact that this state of neglect did in fact exist. There was serious disagreement, however, about what to do about the working class alienation from the church that had resulted from this neglect—and this disagreement about evangelization is at the very heart of the novel.

The fictional parish of Saint-Marc has 38,000 people living within its borders. Sixty-five percent of these people are factory workers and their families and only 1.5% of them practice their religion. The pastor, abbé

Florian, has a heart condition and is pacing himself in order to complete the biography of an obscure priest whom he would like to see canonized by the church. He has all but given up any attempt to bring the Christian message to his parishioners and has retreated into the safety of personal and private piety. Thus, the real work of evangelization is carried on by two younger men, les pères Barré and Reismann, whose dedication and sense of vocation are lauded from one end of the novel to the other. As far as the third person narrative voice of this novel is concerned, they are genuine apostles who eat very little, live in simplicity and poverty, and devote all their energies to their work. As might be expected, they get along very well with the local Communist politicians and are attempting to project to the working class people in the area a new image of the church and clergy. This explains in part why their Roman collar has been replaced by a turtleneck sweater, the eccleciastical word "paroisse" has been replaced by the neutral and secular sounding "secteur," the statues have been removed from the church and sold, and the main altar has been replaced by a stark looking glass cube.

Into this situation, Saint Pierre thrusts thirty year old Paul Delance. Having recently served as an assistant to an auxiliary bishop, and sincerely wondering if he might be better suited for life in a monastery where he could devote his whole life to prayer and meditation far from the world's distractions, le père Delance comes to Saint-Marc with good will. At the same time, however, given his mystical temperament, he is ill-equipped to adapt himself to the new apostolate that Barré and his cohorts are in the process of developing. The "old church," with its veneration of the saints and devotion to the Blessed Virgin, its Latin mass and its emphasis on personal spirituality, no longer exists at Saint-Marc. In fact, things have changed so much that Paul soon learns that Barré and Reismann have begun to practice what they call "charité sélective," according to which those members of the parish who come from a bourgeois background are encouraged to go elsewhere. They do this because they feel that the "new church" of solidarity with workers cannot come into being until the last vestiges of social privilege are eradicated.

This struggle between the old and the new is presented dramatically at the beginning of the novel during a funeral mass. A former army officer is being eulogized not by his old friend, the abbé Florian, who is ill, but by Barré. When the latter seizes upon this opportunity to condemn the church's outdated approval of chivalry, as well as the concept of the just war with its mystical and nationalistic overtones, a layman, Georges

Gallart, becomes so exasperated that he rises during Barré's sermon and interrupts him by asking that the congregation, angry at this attack upon their deceased friend, join him in reciting the Lord's Prayer. Barré is upset, but yields in order to carry on his campaign for change at another time in more favorable circumstances. Gallart, a Norman like so many of Saint Pierre's heroes, is a scientist and university professor who, in his fifties, finds himself returning to the faith of his youth. He seems to represent, throughout the novel, a point of view regarding the changes taking place at Saint-Marc, that Saint Pierre, in his work and public pronouncements as a polemicist, would approve of. As we shall see, however, Gallart is anything but a one-dimensional character. For although he can at times be an eloquent spokesman for certain values of the old church, one can also be suspicious about his motives. In any case, Gallart as a character serves as a tangible link between Saint Pierre's work and that of predecessors such as Léon Bloy, Charles Péguy, and, especially, Bernanos.

This novel, like the earlier ones, is more powerful for its successful creation of atmosphere than for its story line. In fact, as usual, the plot is quite simple, for through a series of confrontations between characters, we come to understand more deeply the differences between the old church and the new church. When, by the end of the novel, eccleciastical authorities decide that Barré and Reismann have gone too far in certain respects, they are transferred to a new assignment. Barré, convinced of the rectitude of his position, accepts the change of duties in order to continue to press for the vindication of his point of view. Reismann, on the other hand, is a weaker and more naive individual who finally yields to the temptation to live with Madeleine, a young atheist who has befriended him. His faith is now completely centered on social progress, and his ideal world is one in which people will not suffer alone and children will not die. He has left the church.

To reduce the novel to the bare bones of its story line is of course to do it a severe injustice, for it is rich in complexity and contains a number of striking sub-themes. As mentioned above, the theme of the clash between the old and the new church is crucial to the novel and we shall have more to say about it later. But one of the things that makes the portrayal of this clash so striking is the sociological, theological, and psychological background that is presented as a backdrop to this central tension.

First, from a sociological point of view, the fictional "new town" of Villedieu is not really a "ville," or a town in the traditional French sense, nor do its inhabitants have much of an understanding of the notion of the divine in their lives. Rather, it is what R.-M Albérès calls "un des échecs de la civilisation française du XXe siècle, un de ces monstres invertébrés, une sorte de leucocyte devenu fou et rejeté loin de Paris."[3] In an attempt in postwar France to remedy the nation's chronic housing shortage, successive governments under the Fourth and Fifth Republics embarked upon a program of constructing large, low-cost, and mostly public owned and operated, housing projects. Usually built in areas where slums had previously existed, they had as one of their goals the relocation of the inhabitants of this substandard housing into more salubrious surroundings. But somewhere along the line something went wrong, for such projects, called H.L.M. (Habitations à Loyer Modéré), tended to take the form of multistory dwellings and were not properly insulated to provide quiet and privacy for their inhabitants. Furthermore, the overall landscape in which they were built was generally less than ideal, so that the inhabitants of these new communities often felt frustration with and alienation from their surroundings. Uprooted from their admittedly substandard slum dwelling, which often lacked even the basics in terms of sanitary facilities, they found themselves transplanted to buildings that did in fact provide such basic amenities, but in which everything else—like the neighborhood café, bakery, school, and local landmarks—was omitted.

Saint Pierre, although hardly a socialist, nevertheless writes of the conditions in which these poor people live in a manner that reminds us of Zola. The narrator's voice is indignant at such shabby living conditions and resounds with sympathy for the poor. In the opening scene of the novel, Paul Delance, walking through the cemetery of Villedieu, looks out at the town around him and notes in a glance the old homes and the construction of the new ones that are to take their place:

> Au-delà du clocher gothique, les jardins potagers et les arbres fruitiers d'un quartier condamné à mort: victimes prochaines des architectes—si l'on peut ainsi nommer les auteurs responsables des "grands ensembles immobiliers" comme ils disent. Car ces cavernes sonores, ces falaises habitées, ces ruches plates et monstrueuses allaient bientôt remplacer les quelques ombres et les quelques sentiers ou l'œil se reposait encore. (18)

Later, Paul will get to know many of the people who live in the parish, including many who have never attended church, for he systematically goes through the housing projects, ringing people's door bells and asking if he can be of help. Gradually, through his own conversations with the inhabitants of the town, as well as through the narrator's voice and those of other characters, the reader comes to understand that Villedieu is merely a variant on the image that opens the novel: that of the cemetery. It is dead and the people who reside in it are spiritually moribund.

Georges Gallart, talking to le père Le Virioux, who is the pastor of the neighboring Sainte-Céline parish, is impressed by what the latter has accomplished, utilizing volunteer labor, in helping people to improve their living conditions. Despite this success, Le Virioux harbors no illusions. While conceding that he has accomplished a number of tangible, concrete goals, he cannot hide his disappointment at his lack of success in preaching the gospel:

> Oh, je ne me fais pas d'illusions! Les conversions marchent beaucoup mieux chez les Gitans, les chiffonniers et les clochards que dans les milieux ouvriers. Et j'en ai beaucoup, des ouvriers, à Sainte-Céline. Ils n'offrent guère de prise à l'Evangile . . . Allons! Nous sommes dans un monde qui a voulu exiler Dieu et que l'amour n'irrigue plus . . . Le marxisme a semé le sable, il a brûlé la terre pour que le Christ n'ait plus Sa moisson, ni le prêtre sa gerbe d'âmes . . . . (183)

Obviously, this sociological dimension, the futility of attempting to convert people who already have a religion, Marxism, is intimately linked to the theological dimension of the novel. But the full importance of the theological truth, or message, imbedded in the text, only becomes fully apparent near the end of the novel in a scene that describes a meeting of thirty-one priests involved in working among the suburban proletariat. Although they have come together to discuss pastoral problems, it soon becomes evident to Paul Delance that theology has taken a back seat to Marxist analysis among most of these men. For not only do they no longer dress like priests, they do not even talk like priests. One priest takes the microphone and urges his colleagues to encourage workers to push for more material benefits. He argues that although workers enjoy better living and working conditions than they did twenty years ago, it is the job of the Action Catholique Ouvrière to urge them to demand even more material benefits. At the same time, he tells his listeners to exclude from their concern anyone who belongs to the "patronal" class. Paul Delance sits quietly and listens while other priests speak up, often expressing themselves through the use of slang and vulgarities in imitation of the working class people among whom they work. But if Paul Delance can contain his frustration, the narrator's voice cannot:

> A ce relâchement dans le langage, correspondait un relâchement tragique dans la spiritualité. Pas une seule fois, l'un des vingt jeunes prêtres qui restaient là n'y proposa une solution touchant l'indifférence religieuse du monde ouvrier, cette fuite oblique devant la parole de Dieu, l'invasion du matérialisme et le désert des âmes. (259)

Finally, at the end of the meeting, Paul cannot keep himself from speaking and when he does it is to defend the traditional Catholic position on the preaching of the gospel. First, no matter what, he does not want to exclude anyone from hearing the divine message as one of love: "Je n'irai pas chercher l'âme ouvrière dans sa révolte. J'irai la chercher dans son amour" (264). Secondly, priests are neither politicians nor social workers: "Nous ne devons jamais prendre directement en charge les problèmes temporels—car le Christ ne l'a jamais fait" (265). And finally, the only thing that they are to condemn is sin, as reflected in "le matérialisme sous toutes ses formes—y compris le matérialisme des pauvres" (265).

It should be obvious that the vehicle used by Saint Pierre to make both his socio-political and theological points is Paul Delance. Paul, who, as mentioned earlier, has been sent to this working class parish in order to learn more about the world, is nothing less than the subject of a *Bildungsroman*. At the beginning of the novel he arrives somewhat innocent and unsuspecting of what the worker priests of the Paris area are involved in, and by the end of the novel he will have received a complete education in this regard. But, significantly, his own faith is not shattered in the process. Instead, he finds that his compassion for the poor and the exploited grows considerably. But this personal growth in his understanding of the spirit of poverty does not cause him to break off relations with people from other social and economic backgrounds.

In the end, Paul's real development, as he faces the materialism that surrounds him, is of a mystical nature. More and more, as the novel unfolds, we find him, not unlike the curé d'Ars, involuntarily developing a following as a person with mystical powers. From neighboring towns, as well as from Paris itself, people come to have him hear their confession.

Long hours devoted to close exposure to Satan's work have exhausted him. When he tells the abbé Florian that he has not said his mass for the past two days, he tries to explain why: "Et je ne l'ai pas célébrée, parce que je n'en suis pas digne—et parce que je n'ai plus la force" (293). But Florian counsels patience and prudence, telling him not to give up his daily mass, which is the basis of his spiritual life, despite his feelings of unworthiness. Delance seems to agree and promises to take better care of himself.

In the final scene of the novel, Paul is locked in combat with Satan in the confessional as Sophie Lipari, formerly Georges Gallart's mistress, waits outside to talk to him. This conversation, like so many others in the novel, is redolent of various aspects of Bernanos's fictional universe. Like the abbé Donissan in *Sous le soleil de Satan* (1926) and the curé d'Ambricourt in *Journal d'un curé de campagne* (1936), Paul Delance has the ability to read into people's souls. The conversation with Sophie, like the pivotal one between the Countess and the Curé in *Journal d'un curé de campagne*, involves the interaction between a priest with mystical powers and a woman who is spiritually paralyzed by the power of Satan. One thinks of Jesus meeting the woman at the well or encountering Mary Magdelan for the first time. In each case, the priest attempts to open the woman to the power of divine love. In the case of the Countess, the curé d'Ambricourt wants her to abandon her hatred of God whom she holds responsible for the death of her son. Here, Sophie is in despair because she has been abandoned by her lover who, in turn, has rediscovered religious faith. She is thus seeking love, but Delance tells her that real love is much larger and more powerful than that provided by one individual: "L'essentiel est de savoir que l'amour de Dieu est autour de vous. C'est un fait, Madame, un fait violent. Il est là, mille fois plus fort que le désir d'un homme" (308-09). As they talk, and as the novel ends, it is obvious that Paul is enjoying some kind of mystical vision which Sophie is unable to share, but to which she is nonetheless a witness. In this closing scene, Saint Pierre seems to be trying to show his reader the limits of grace, which is now bestowed upon Paul in abundance, but denied to Sophie, whose heart is open only to human love, since it is the only kind she knows about. Paul's vision, purely spiritual, is also in marked contrast to the opening vision of the novel, the one in which Paul visits the cemetery of Villedieu and contemplates with sadness the tombs and gravestones: "Et toute cette quincaillerie, cette architecture et ces caprices funéraires s'étendaient sur des centaines de mètres, avec une sorte d'acharnement dans la laideur, témoins d'une civilisation sans génie, sans humour et sans panache" (18). For just as he had been tempted to ask himself then "Où est la douceur de la mort," so now he can think and talk of nothing but death as expressed through the notions of silence and perfect union with God. In reminiscence of St. John of the Cross, he calls out, as Sophie listens, "Mon Seigneur et mon Dieu, souvenez-vous: dès le jour où je vous ai vu, je suis devenu tel que rien ici-bas ne pourra me contenter une heure" (312). But the last line of the novel, reminding us of the title of Bernanos's first novel, *Sous le soleil de Satan*, reveals finally what this scene is all about: "N'ayant jamais rien vu—jamais—qui ressemblât aux traits de Paul à ce moment, Sophie contemplait avec stupeur un visage d'homme sous le soleil de Dieu" (313). In stark contrast to the Bernanosian vision of man as a creature being permanently stalked by Satan, Saint Pierre here wants to show us a more optimistic view of the human condition. Grace aiding, a real priest is one who leads a deep spiritual life. Delance is first and foremost a holy man and only secondarily an organizer, administrator, or preacher.

If we define the Catholic novel as one in which the author's faith is a factor in the creation of the work and, more importantly, one in which the author deliberately attempts to bring to life for his reader the notion of the supernatural in human affairs, *Les Nouveaux Prêtres* (along with its sequel *La Passion de l'abbé Delance*) is probably the most Catholic of Saint Pierre's novels. In writing such a novel, however, the author must be subtle and ought not disturb the secular reader's sense of *vraisemblance*. That is, events with potent supernatural dimensions to them, like the Countess's change of heart in her conversation with the curé d'Ambricourt in *Journal d'un curé de campagne* and her subsequent fatal heart attack, or the conversion of Louis in Mauriac's *Nœud de vipères* (1933), must also be able to be understood on a different level by those who are without faith. This ability to function on both levels, that is, to imply strongly the active operation of invisible powers while remaining comprehensible to eyes that do not acknowledge such powers, is essential to the success of the modern Catholic novel, and in my view Saint Pierre succeeds in *Les Nouveaux Prêtres* in adroitly creating character and incident on both levels of meaning. Paul's final vision is one thing to Sophie, who is full of human love for Gallart but as yet untouched by divine grace, but something entirely different to a reader with a Christian sensitivity. Of all his novels, this one takes the greatest artistic risks and, concomitantly, enjoys the greatest success.

No discussion of *Les Nouveaux Prêtres* could be complete without reference to the controversy that it created in both religious and literary circles. The first broadside against the novel came from the abbé Georges Michonneau, who for years had been involved in the working class apostolate. Writing in the liberal and left-leaning weekly *Témoignage Chrétien*, to which Saint Pierre himself had contributed regularly for eight years (1946-54), Michonneau attacked Saint Pierre for "diffamation" of the French clergy. "Vous dites: le clergé français est atteint de progressisme, soit par conviction, soit par complicité. Et cela veut dire que le clergé de France n'a pris aucunement en considération les avertissements des papes. Quelle calomnie." He then goes on to point out—correctly—that in the novel it is Barré and Reismann, and not Paul Delance, who devote themselves tirelessly to acts of charity on behalf of the poor:

> Ce n'est pas Delance qui soigne le vieux Kleber silicosé, ce n'est pas lui qui pleure le petit Pedro. Ce n'est pas lui qui voit le Christ écrasé dans la chair et dans l'âme avilie des travailleurs. Ce n'est pas lui qui communie à leur soif de justice, de dignité, de paix . . . Ce sont les autres, justement.[4]

As Michonneau's words indicate, he recognized in the novel that the "prêtres progressistes" are presented as authentic apostles. The novelist may or may not personally think that they have gone too far into the Marxist camp, but his opinion is of no consequence for the simple reason that these characters have taken on a life of their own. Michonneau's observation in this regard, that they are truly the most charitable priestly characters in the novel, is (inadvertently on his part) the best proof of this fact. In other words, the narrator's voice has given them credit for what they are doing, although it has expressed concern about their style, the way in which they do things. Now, some twenty-five years later, when we can easily put aside all the emotion that was involved in this public debate, the essence of the problem seems to have been that Michonneau felt that Saint Pierre was labeling as Communists all priests working among the de-Christianized working class poor of the "red belt" communes outside Paris. He ends his vitriolic essay by writing: "Vous, M. de Saint Pierre, vous nous traitez de prêtres communistes. . . ," even though this expression does not appear once in the novel. There can be no doubt that Saint Pierre personally thought that what the novel's narrative voice calls the "prêtres progressistes" are clearly overly sympathetic to the Communists and even lapse at times into the use of Communist terminology, but in the novel they are never specifically called Communists. In any case, as a result of this article, Saint Pierre and his publisher, Editions de la Table Ronde, brought a lawsuit against *Témoignage Chrétien* for having been guilty of making "des implications qui portent atteinte à leur honneur et à leur considération."[5] The suit did not name the abbé Michonneau, out of respect for his priestly office, but it did name both *Témoignage Chrétien* and its publisher Georges Montaron. Faced with the scandal of Christians fighting with each other in public, Mgr. Veuillot, Archbishop of Paris, asked both parties to cease and desist. As a result, Saint Pierre finally agreed to drop the suit when the abbé Michonneau offered to make a public statement in which he assured Saint Pierre that "il s'excusait des termes qui auraient pu porter atteinte à son honneur d'écrivain chrétien. Il retire les expressions qu'il a employées à son egard et à l'égard de ses lecteurs et lui exprime ses regrets, affirmant publiquement qu'il ne doute pas de la sincérité de ses intentions."[6]

Rereading the documents involved in this controversy at a distance of twenty-five years, one cannot help but be struck by the fact that Michonneau's objections are principally ideological and not literary. Since Saint Pierre's name had already been associated with right-wing causes, most notably the retention of Algeria as a French colony under the rallying cry of "Algérie Française," and then the amnesty campaign for those military men who had tried, in 1961, to overthrow De Gaulle's government as a final desperate gesture to hold on to Algeria, it was assumed in advance by Michonneau that the novel would be ideologically unacceptable to progressive and liberal Catholics. The novel is in fact much more nuanced and balanced than Michonneau gives it credit for being. Totally lacking in his analysis of it, is any appreciation of the fact that the character who speaks out the most vehemently against these new progressive priests, the layman Georges Gallart, is also a personal hypocrite who exploits the love and affection of a woman, Sophie Lipari, without giving anything in return. In comparison to Gallart, le père Barré emerges as a generous Christian who, unlike Gallart, practices what he preaches. Thus, despite the fact that Michonneau makes the point in his article that the "prêtres progressistes" in the novel are the ones who show real devotion to the poor and sick, he still seems to be so blinded by dislike of Saint Pierre that he cannot draw the obvious conclusion: these priests behave the way they do because, in this novel, they are portrayed as real Christians. Another point that close examination of the novel would have revealed to the abbé Michonneau is that Paul Delance, although he does experience spiritual growth in the course of the novel, is evidently not the best suited priest to engage in this sort of urban mission. Despite what Saint Pierre's intentions might have been with respect to this character, Delance does live a life of his own, and as the reader analyzes his temperament and personality it becomes clear that Barré—and to a lesser extent Reismann—are much better suited to the urban apostolate than is Delance. In the past twenty-five years, the "excesses" that Barré is guilty of—such as talking on a personal basis to Communists (and sometimes sounding like them when he talks) or making a personal preferential option for the welfare of poor people—have become part and parcel of Catholicism, especially in underdeveloped countries and in poverty-stricken and de-Christianized places like the fictional Villedieu. If anything, Barré's ideological positions seem in retrospect to be mild to us today. But at the same time, the central theme of the novel, which revolves around a definition of the spiritual life in a time of rapid social change and of ideological crisis, is more than ever potent and of contemporary interest.

The second major public quarrel over the novel took place with the Catholic novelist Gilbert Cesbron, who attacked Saint Pierre in *Le Figaro*.[7] Cesbron, whose celebrated novel, *Les Saints vont en enfer* (1952), had dealt with the same general theme, the apostolate of worker priests in the same "red belt" towns depicted in Saint Pierre's fictional Villedieu, sought to come to the aid of the abbé Michonneau and, in so doing, referred to Saint Pierre and the so-called "intégriste" Catholics like him as the church's spoiled children: "les enfants gâtés de l'église."

To Cesbron, whose novel about the first generation of worker priests had revealed itself to be deeply sympathetic to both the men and their mission, people like Saint Pierre are essentially hypocrites because they claim to support the forces of order, authority, and hierarchy. But now that the post-conciliar church has changed its stance and its tone of voice, these same "spoiled children" attack order, authority, and hierarchy and defend their action by claiming that far too many priests and bishops have been soiled by Marxist influences. He accuses Saint Pierre of lumping several quite different issues together and, if anyone disagrees with him on a given issue, of smearing that person by accusing him of naiveté at best and, at worst, Marxist delusions. The major political issues mentioned by Cesbron—"l'Algérie française, l'antigaullisme, l'amnistie, le Concile, l'Eglise de France,"—are of course not all raised in the novel (only the last two are), but Cesbron's obstinacy in condemning the novel for political reasons reflects quite well the passion that the book had aroused.

A more specific objection raised by Cesbron is built on the Parable of the Lost Sheep. To him, the French bourgeois Catholic is one of the ninety-nine sheep already in the fold, and his duty is to bring the last sheep, the lost one, into the fold. To Cesbron, this need to evangelize the working class is an imperious priority, especially since, in the present-day working class population, "pour une seule fidèle, il y a 99 brebis perdues." He also compares French bourgeois Catholics to "les ouvriers de la première heure et le frère aîné de l'Enfant prodigue." If they are not in fact already saved, they have at least received the news of salvation, whereas France's de-Christianized masses have not. While Cesbron does not go so far as to condone what Saint Pierre calls in the novel the "charité sélective" exercised by Fathers Barré and Reismann, he does not deny that this phenomenon exists.

In summary, Cesbron is making valid points with which no sincere Christian can disagree. At the same time, his points have little to do directly with the novel, which is in fact much more sympathetic to the "new priests" than he or his liberal supporters were willing to admit. Thus, once again, we see that the novel was attacked or lauded not so much on its own faults or merits, as because Saint Pierre's name was on the title page. At the time, Saint Pierre associated with so many political causes that appealed to a small but highly committed group of voters on the right end of the political spectrum, that spontaneous condemnation of the novel by political enemies should not be difficult to understand. In conclusion, Cesbron ends his article with an emotional call to Saint Pierre to drop his libel suit against the abbé Michonneau: "Mais ce procès n'aura pas lieu, n'est-ce pas?—Ou alors, Michel de Saint Pierre, ne prétendez plus jamais défendre l'honneur de Dieu."

Saint Pierre, seemingly as anxious to take advantage of an opportunity to generate further publicity for his novel as to defend his honor and reputation, demanded and received from *Le Figaro* the right to respond to Cesbron's article.[8] He focuses on two major points raised by his adversary: the idea that a bourgeois writer, as a "spoiled child" of the church, should not impose his own standards and preconceived notions on a working class situation, and the need for obedience on the part of conservative

Catholics to accept the decisions of Vatican II instead of attempting to sabotage them.

On the first point, he reminds Cesbron that for six years he had earned his living by working with his hands. For this reason, he feels that he has the right to treat working class life in his novels. Furthermore, Saint Pierre urges that priests, instead of taking a sociological approach to their ministry, including going so far as to eliminate from consideration the "spoiled children" of the traditional bourgeoisie, should follow Saint Paul's dictum and attempt to be all things to all people: "Soyez tout à tous." Obviously, such an attitude, even interpreted in the manner of Saint Pierre, would not automatically preclude evangelization that takes local circumstances into consideration. Finally, Saint Pierre claims that it is the "progressistes" within the church who are disobeying church law and flagrantly ignoring church doctrine, while the traditionalists like himself are merely trying to preserve the church from forgetting its past in its mad dash to assimilate to the values of a secular, materialistic, and Marxist-influenced society.

The third major exchange about the novel took place in reaction to Pierre-Henri Simon's review of it in *Le Monde*. While Simon conceded that a good novel can be written about an emotionally charged contemporary subject, he nonetheless expressed grave reservations about *Les Nouveaux Prêtres*. He depicts Saint Pierre as an ideologue who wants to turn back the clock and keep the clergy from attempting to use new methods to win back to the church the de-Christianized working class French masses. While granting that "l'auteur des *Aristocrates* et des *Murmures de Satan* a une vivacité d'écriture et parfois une gravité d'esprit qui peuvent retenir aussi les lecteurs exigeants,"[9] he still feels that the novel fails because the ideology that it communicates all too vividly—questioning the new style of apostolate and calling for a return to pre-conciliar methods—is overtly transparent and not rooted subtly enough in the characters. To Simon, ideology in a novel must be "traitée d'une façon dramatique, intime, existentielle: non pas vue du dehors et débattue théoriquement, mais incarnée dans la subjectivité des personnages, mêlée à leur vie intérieure et portée à ce niveau profond où elle touche pour chacun à des options risquées et fondamentales." To Simon, as for Michonneau and other liberal Catholic critics, the heart of the problem is that the depiction of Barré verges on caricature. Typical of such objections, Simon asks: "A supposer que des cas aussi abérrants existent, est-il équitable de définir par eux, et par eux seuls, le style du nouvel apostolat?" The answer is obviously negative as far as P.-H. Simon is concerned, because he interprets the novel as one that takes a stand against "l'événement énorme qui représente l'effort de l'Eglise conciliaire pour rentrer dans le monde moderne en mettant à jour la formulation de sa doctrine et le style de sa pastorale."

As might be expected, Saint Pierre, not one to miss an opportunity to generate publicity for one of his novels, demanded the right to respond to Simon's review. *Le Monde*, although unaccustomed to making such a gesture, nonetheless decided to print Saint Pierre's letter so that he could not claim that his voice was being "etouffé" by his adversaries.[10] One interesting point about the letter is that *Le Monde* claimed that it took Saint Pierre over four months to write in defense of his novel, thereby giving rise to the suspicion that the novelist's letter of protest was merely another publicity stunt designed to keep his name before the public. As a preface to Saint Pierre's letter of response, the newspaper printed a long preamble which included the following statement:

> L'abus de droit paraît ici flagrant. Quel auteur, quel artiste, ne s'est senti un jour ou l'autre plus ou moins incompris? L'un et l'autre savent pourtant qu'en rendant leur œuvre publique ils la soumettent du même coup au jugement de chacun, et plus particulièrement à celui des critiques. Le législateur de 1881 qui instituait le droit de réponse, correctif nécessaire à la liberté de la presse, n'entendait certainement pas abolir celle-ci en permettant à tout auteur justement déçu ou assoiffé de publicité de prodiguer à son gré explications et protestations.[11]

As for Saint Pierre's response, it seems halfhearted, and in fact the whole first half of it, devoted to the curé d'Ars, has nothing to do directly with Simon's review. Finally, in the second half of his letter he addresses the question that Simon had focused on in his review and claims categorically that Barré and Reismann are not distortions: "J'ai voulu dire que le mal, *s'il n'est pas encore général*, est partout et *étendu*. Mes abbés Barré, Reismann, quoi qu'en ait dit une certaine presse, sous la plume de gens qui sans doute se sentaient 'touchés,' ne sont pas des cas exceptionnels." Thus, we see here once again that the center of concern in both the attack on the novel and Saint Pierre's defense of it resides in the question of the new apostolate and the real living people involved in it. The rejection of the novel by Michonneau (and to a lesser extent by Simon) is inspired in large part by their desire to defend the Council and to free the clergy to come to grips with the world in new and imaginative ways. Since *Les Nouveaux Prêtres* obviously questions that new direction, Saint Pierre's critics concluded that it was a poorly written novel. In the process of defending himself (and we should not be naive enough to believe that Saint Pierre did not want to generate publicity for his book in demanding his so-called "right of response,") against ideological and nonliterary attacks, Saint Pierre allowed himself to abandon his claim to being a creative artist. In so doing he abetted his adversaries by implicitly granting their major point that the novel was merely a *roman à thèse*, and not a more complex work designed to make an enduring statement in an artful manner. For the rest of his career, *Le Monde* would never again review any of his books. Upon his death, however, they did publish a sympathetic article about his overall achievement as a writer and spokesman for traditionalist Catholic concerns.[12]

The controversy that this novel created at the time of publication is no doubt responsible in part for the neglect from which it has suffered in the intervening years. In retrospect, the very title, *Les Nouveaux Prêtres*, was a double-edged sword. If, on the one hand, it easily lent itself to the public imagination and in the process no doubt helped to spur sales of the book, it was also widely misunderstood. In the last twenty years, as France has rushed headlong into modernity, movements of various kinds have been called "new" by various commentators. In the mid-sixties when *Les Nouveaux Prêtres* appeared, "la nouvelle vague" in film was already well established and "la nouvelle critique" was in the process of coming to public attention. And of course, "la nouvelle cuisine," "les nouveaux philosophes" and "le nouveau théâtre" were not far off. With reference to Saint Pierre, however, after having published novels with pluralized, all-encompassing titles like *Les Aristocrates* and *Les Ecrivains*, he then published *Les Nouveaux Aristocrates* as well as *La Nouvelle Race*, a reportage containing the results of the many interviews with teenagers that had been used as a basis for *Les Nouveaux Aristocrates*. Only Gilbert Ganne in *L'Aurore* seems to have been able to bring out clearly Saint Pierre's intentions in choosing the title for *Les Nouveaux Prêtres*. In an interview that appeared at the time of the book's publication, Ganne asked Saint Pierre if the use of the adjective "new" in yet another novel was related to the fact that *Les Nouveaux Aristocrates*, three years earlier, had sold 100,000 copies. Saint Pierre responded:

Les Nouveaux Aristocrates ont été suivis, en effet, par *La Nouvelle Race* et aujourd'hui par *Les Nouveaux Prêtres*. Mais de quoi s'agit-il? Successivement de l'élite, de la jeunesse et des clercs. C'est-à-dire que j'achève aujourd'hui le triptyque que j'ai voulu consacrer à ce que j'appelle "les mutants." J'ai eté très frappé par une réponse qu'un jeune a faite, un jour à un enquêteur: "Aujourd'hui, on change de siècle tous les dix ans. . ." Pour moi, il ne s'agit donc plus d'évolution, mais de mutation. En ce qui concerne *Les Nouveaux Aristocrates*, par exemple, l'ancienne élite ne peut absolument pas se reconnaître dans la nouvelle élite.[13]

Thus, there should be no question of considering priests like Barré and Reismann as evil people trying to destroy a church that should not change. Rather, they should be considered as representatives of change in a world that changed so rapidly from 1955 to 1965 that the "nouvelle élite" of which they are emblematic bore virtually no resemblance to the traditional elite that had preceded it. Elsewhere in the same interview, more light is shed on this same question, for Saint Pierre makes it clear that he is for change both in the church and in society at large. He expresses to Ganne his "aspiration au progrès qui peut nous animer tous," as well as "le sentiment que nous éprouvons d'une évolution nécessaire." But, he adds, this is only the normal process of change that is to be expected, even encouraged. It differs from "progressisme" which he characterizes as the "impatience de détruire," and the "progressiste" himself as a "réformateur trop hâtif."

Thus, in the final analysis, we are talking about degree and not essence. It is clear in the novel that Jules Barré is a dedicated, clean living and hard working churchman. At the time, however, because the book was published in the very midst of the changes that it was describing, it was difficult to see it for what it was: an attempt by a Catholic novelist to deal with the problem of the sacred in a secular society by using the materials that he had at hand. *Les Nouveaux Prêtres* is just as important as a Catholic novel of the sixties as *Nœud de vipères* and *Journal d'un curé de campagne* were for earlier generations. Like Mauriac and Bernanos, Saint Pierre was attempting to create in his reader's mind an appreciation for the spiritual realities hidden beneath the concrete facade of everyday reality. Also, like them, he was attempting to write a novel that could be understood on both a secular and a spiritual level. Are Paul Delance's mystical experiences real or are they illusions? It is ultimately up to each reader to decide this question, but the novel does in fact raise the question, which is one thing that a Catholic novel should do.

Thus, when Robert Kanters, who reviewed the novel for *Le Figaro*, officiously declared that "l'œuvre de Michel de Saint Pierre marque une régression du roman catholique par rapport aux œuvres des Mauriac et des Bernanos,"[14] it is essential to note that his reasons had nothing to do with literature and everything to do with politics. In fact, his conclusion is not even drawn from his discussion of the novel, which is generally positive, but from his image of Saint Pierre as an ultraconservative. After all, since in Kanters's mind, Saint Pierre "invective pêle-mêle contre les intellectuels sartrisants, les libéraux à lunettes et les cinéastes érotiques, ou bien prête généreusement au Diable la devise de Descartes," he must be a low-grade novelist. As narrow-minded as Kanters's view is, it is unfortunately rather typical. To expect Saint Pierre to have written a Catholic novel in the mid-sixties, just as Vatican II was coming to an end, that would be concerned with the same problems (treated in a simple way) as the novels that Mauriac and Bernanos had published in the interwar years, is a short-sighted view, to say the least.

In conclusion, *Les Nouveaux Prêtres* is long overdue for resurrection and re-evaluation. Like Pascal's *Lettres Provinciales*, it cried out against contemporary abuses and suggested corrective measures. Unlike that work, however, it was not published anonymously. Thus, the novelist's political enemies found their best defense in attacking the man rather than his work. Although passions on both sides of the issues raised in the novel have not completely subsided, it should be possible today to discuss *Les Nouveaux Prêtres* more rationally as a serious attempt to write a Catholic novel in an age of intense and painful change, employing as the subject of that novel the very changes taking place in society. *Les Nouveaux Prêtres* is not only one of Saint Pierre's two or three best novels, it is also a courageous and largely successful attempt to contribute to the tradition of the modern Catholic novel in the sixties.

6. The Novelist As Witness to His Age

SIX YEARS INTERVENED BETWEEN THE PUBLICATION OF *LES NOUVEAUX Prêtres* and Saint Pierre's next novel, *Le Milliardaire*.[1] In the interim, a slight change seems to have taken place in his mind with regard to his view of his work. At the time of publication of *Les Nouveaux Prêtres,* he still saw himself as an "écrivain chrétien," but by the time the decade came to an end, he was defining himself primarily as an "écrivain témoin de son temps." The two terms are not mutually exclusive, and Bernanos and Mauriac are both emblematic in this respect. During their careers, they both wrote pamphlets and newspaper articles in which they commented on the problems afflicting the era in which they lived. Their witnessing extended even to their private correspondence, for as Jean Murray, the editor of Bernanos's correspondence, reminds us: "Maintes lettres révèlent combien Bernanos prenait au sérieux le rôle de témoin de son temps."[2] The difference between these earlier writers and Saint Pierre is that the latter wants to be a witness not only in his pamphlets and public statements, but also in his novels. It is the novels themselves that henceforth will be more the work of an "écrivain témoin de son temps" than of an "écrivain chrétien."

A year after the success of *Les Nouveaux Prêtres*, we find Saint Pierre pondering his role as a writer and asking whether a novelist's work should vividly reflect the tensions of contemporary life. He writes: "Le problème se trouve ainsi clairement posé au romancier. Doit-il être témoin de son temps? Doit-il au contraire prendre du recul, rester volontairement inactuel?" His answer to this rhetorical question was predictable: "Pour ma part, touchant le problème du témoignage, il m'apparaît que nous devons verser notre pièce au débat, dans la période d'histoire confuse, dramatique et passionnante que nous traversons. . . ."[3] Two years later, as he was deeply involved in writing his two-volume history of the Romanovs, we find him still thinking about his vocation and about the direction that his future work will take. Characterizing *Les Nouveaux Prêtres* and the three works that he published in rapid succession after it, *Sainte Colère* (1965), *Ces Prêtres qui souffrent* (1966), and *J'étais à Fatima* (1967), as a "cycle religieux," he tells Jean Montalbetti in an interview: "J'ai d'abord écrit un roman et puis, sous forme de dossiers, j'ai voulu apporter mes preuves. Mais j'ai tenu à terminer ce cycle avec un ouvrage concret, plus positif: c'est ce témoignage sur Fatima." Looking to the future, that is, beyond the historical work on the Romanovs, he already had plans for a new series of novels written in response to the changing nature of society: "Je reviendrai au roman dans trois livres inspirés successivement par les milliardaires, les facultés et la profession médicale." These three novels would be *Le Milliardaire* (1970), *Laurent* (1980), and *Docteur Erikson* (1982). The reason for this new orientation was because

> quand on aborde des professions et des vocations éternelles on atteint un certain côté intemporel. J'ai dû paraître pessimiste dans mes derniers livres, mais en réalité notre univers me passionne à cause de ses mutations. Nous sommes dans la position inconfortable d'un homme qui serait assis entre deux mondes. Le monde nouveau se cache derrière le monde ancien, comme un enfant derrière le dos d'un veillard. Le rôle du romancier est de capter ces mutations au fur et à mesure qu'elles s'opèrent. A la différence de Balzac ou de Zola, nous n'avons pas le temps de nous arrêter devant la contemplation et l'observation minutieuse du monde, sinon les mutations nous échappent. C'est le rythme qui a changé, non la vie. Le romancier d'aujourd'hui, enchaîné à ce mouvement, est contraint de prendre des risques, mais il doit réserver à ses livres le minimum de caractère intemporel et d'universalité qui leur permettra de durer.[4]

In less than a year, the events of 1968 would take place and in their wake the vast changes already in movement in French society would accelerate in speed and gain intensity in the coming decade. Saint Pierre, more than any other contemporary French novelist, would be the chronicler of these changes.

The first novel in this new cycle is *Le Milliardaire*. Its title is significant because of its shift from the plural of the earlier novels to what will henceforth be an emphasis on the singular. This is not to say that he loses interest in writing about social "types" or "groups," that is, workers in *Ce Monde ancien*, adolescents in *Les Nouveaux Aristocrates*, or the collective entities indicated by titles such as *Les Aristocrates*, *Les Ecrivains*, and *Les Nouveaux Prêtres*. After all, *Le Milliardaire* of the title can be said to belong to that group of people that the gospels refer to as "the rich," those for whom salvation is difficult because of their wealth. On the other hand, the author is clearly interested in his hero, Georges-H. Fabre-Simmons, as an individual. He is at the center of the novel less as a symbol of wealthy people in general, than as a very special type of wealthy businessman, the kind that was evolving in reaction to the dawn of the computer age and the growth of service industries in France.

Luc Estang called the novel "le roman le plus accompli, le plus brillant, le plus convaincant de M. Michel de Saint Pierre."[5] One reason offered by Estang for this assessment is that he feels that the "imagination du romancier s'exerce sur une solide documentation." This observation is even more striking with the advantage of hindsight, for Saint Pierre succeeded remarkably well in capturing the flavor and feeling of the computer age—especially in view of the fact that the novel was written several years before most people fully appreciated how the computer would change so many everyday ways of doing things. Writing in the late sixties when only a handful of the most forward-looking French businessmen, following the American model, could be aware of how the computer would modify daily living habits in coming years, Saint Pierre shows great expertise in mastering the language and concepts of the computer age and inserting them into a lively novel. This accomplishment is even more striking when we recall how far France was still behind in this area in 1970, and how it would require a reordering of national priorities during the seventies to allow her to catch up. Thus, *Le Milliardaire* is both a psychological study of an individual as well as an analysis of the French computer industry with its haunting sense of purpose: to lead France into the technological future while at the same time looking over its shoulder at its foreign competitors, especially American giants like IBM, before they corner the French market.

A reading of the opening chapter of *Le Milliardaire* makes it easy to see why Saint Pierre can be called the quintessential novelist of life under the Fifth Republic. Here he brings together Marcel Sangalles, the seventy-two year old president of Chantiers et Ateliers Sangalles, a family-owned business for several generations, since 1842, and Georges Fabre-Simmons, the "milliardaire" of the title, one of whose grandmothers was an American, and who is determined to keep American electronics firms from wiping out French competition. Like Jean Dewinter of *Les Murmures de Satan,* he is the founder of his own firm, Compagnie Française d'Electronique et d'Informatique (CFEI). He has now invited Sangalles to an elaborate business lunch in order to propose a merger, a "fusion" of his own company with the electronics component of Sangalles's giant concern. The contrast between the two men is striking. As the living embodiment of the "patron" in the traditional mold, Sangalles is overweight and a gourmand, while Fabre-Simmons is slim and a gourmet. Sangalles is also a smoker who runs his company on instinct, while Fabre-Simmons, a nonsmoker, makes decisions based on numbers generated by his computers.

Sangalles, in his suspicion of the new generation of technocrats coming to the fore in French business and politics, abhors the new elite (often trained in part at American business schools), which shows off its background and connections by the use of English technical terms. "Je ne supporte pas ce snobisme de l'anglais," huffs Sangalles. "On ne parle plus aujourd'hui que de *marketing,* de *gap,* de *hobby,* de *brain-storming,* de *time-sharing,* et de *package deal*" (23). In addition, he claims that the new technocrats do not seem to enjoy their work the way men of his generation still do. Fabre-Simmons, on the other hand, in so far as he is a self-made man who has turned his initial borrowed capital into an immense fortune, is completely in tune with the new ideas penetrating the French business world. He is aware that the computer industry represents the wave of the future and that an American colossus like IBM has an annual budget exceeding that of many of the world's nations. In order to compete with and to blunt this American technological invasion of France, Fabre-Simmons feels that the French too will have to create giant companies of their own. Thus, he has invited Sangalles to lunch in order to discuss the creation of just such a company.

At the end of their three-hour lunch, Sangalles refuses Fabre-Simmons's overture, but one senses that the latter will not be denied in his quest: he is determined to engineer this merger even if Sangalles opposes him. During the remainder of the novel, Fabre-Simmons will devote himself totally (to the neglect of his wife and children) to this hostile takeover of Sangalles's firm. The chief means that he will employ will be the O.P.A., the "offre publique d'achat," which involves buying up the outstanding shares of Sangalles stock held by the public. But what at first seems like a rather forthright and relatively simple procedure, finally reveals itself to be enormously complicated, with much behind the scenes double-dealing and back-stabbing.

The novel is built on counterpoint, with the focus of the action shifting back and forth constantly between Fabre-Simmons's professional and private lives. Each time that he is deeply involved with his work, there is the risk of a phone call from his wife informing him of a looming family crisis. Likewise, on each occasion that he finally succeeds in talking on a personal basis to a member of his family, his mind begins wandering off to thoughts of business maneuvers. Thus, although he is at times physically present to his family, he is psychologically distanced and estranged from them.

We also see this use of counterpoint within the context of Fabre-Simmons's professional life. He sees himself as one of the leaders of French society, a kind of pioneer. As such, he must struggle against both an overweight government bureaucracy and the backward-looking corporate leaders who want the government to pass protectionist legislation that will allow them to hide from American, German, and Japanese competition. "Je me tue à lutter contre des fonctionnaires jacobins et contre un patronat en hibernation," he laments (45). To Fabre-Simmons, the French computer industry, if it is to survive, must unabashedly assume "des dimensions américaines" (37). Citing the example of a successful French truck builder, he points out that the company "travaille à l'américaine—et je commence à croire, Messieurs, qu'il n'y a pas d'autre manière de travailler" (92). Pierre Mazade, his public relations director, as well as a poet in his free time, characterizes his boss as being "européen, planétaire [et] international" (84), and the description is apt. In the past fifteen years, more and more such men have come to the fore in French society, but in 1970 their relative number was not large. Fabre-Simmons is thus both an individual and a representative example of a major phenomenon of French life that is larger than he is and that has far-reaching implications for the nation as a whole.

The action of the novel opens during the spring, for it is the end of the school year and Fabre-Simmons's two children, Roland and Cécile, both of whom are studying law at the new suburban campus at Boisléger, a fictionalized Nanterre, take their exams in the course of the novel. Françoise, who has been his wife for twenty-five years, has plenty of money but no sense of accomplishing anything on her own. Cécile, cynical and determined to succeed, believes in two things: herself and sexual pleasure. Her immediate goal is to obtain her law degree and after that to maintain her independence. She has no intention of ever marrying. It is as if we are meeting Bénédicte, the sister of Denis Prullé-Rousseau of *Les Nouveaux Aristocrates*, a few years later in life. As she sees things, a woman either marries a man with money or without it. If she does the former, she risks becoming a "bibelot de luxe dans la maison." The other possibility is even worse:

> vous épousez un minus, et vous êtes bonne pour cuire le bifteck-frites, faire le ménage, laver les caleçons et torcher les gosses! Non, merci . . . Moi, je veux me réaliser pleinement, jouir de moi-même. Et des autres, bien sûr . . . Je pense qu'il y a donc une troisième solution: ne pas se marier. (195)

Her brother Roland, very much like Denis Prullé-Rousseau and so many of Saint Pierre's other young men in rebellion against society and their families, reflects another aspect of the post-1968 generation: idealistic political action outside of traditional party structures, which are rejected as being part of the problem. Like the student activists at Nanterre during the events of 1968, Roland wants to transport revolution from the university campus into the factories located nearby. He is the leader of a group of Maoists who, at the very gates of the factories, distribute flyers calling upon the workers to sabotage the machinery upon which they work. Among the plants where he has engaged in demonstrations and fought with police is one owned by his father's company. Unlike Cécile, who has done well in school, Roland has spent so much time playing at revolution with his Marxist cellmates that he has not prepared himself adequately for his end of year exams.

The remarkable thing about the portrayal of the Fabre-Simmons children is the degree of sympathy that the author displays for them. Despite their weaknesses and shortcomings, it is obvious that their parents, as well as society at large, share responsibility for their conduct and attitudes. Fabre-Simmons and his wife are both atheists and their reason-for-being is essentially materialistic in nature. Fabre-Simmons seems to live for the satisfaction that he derives from accumulating and exercising power through the use of his money. Joined to this is the excitement generated by being a leader who faces up to the promises and challenges of the future: "Moi, je sais qu'ici, en Europe, je vois plus grand et j'ose plus loin que les autres dans mon domaine. Gérer n'est rien, conserver n'est rien, diriger n'est rien. Ce qui compte, c'est explorer" (270). Devoting his whole life to his work, he has almost no time left for his children. Now, when they need him more than ever, he remains remote.

Françoise, who has had the major responsibility in raising their offspring, shares his atheism. Early in the novel she tells him that she would like him to pay more attention to her and to the children. She wants him to be more loving and caring. When Fabre-Simmons tells her that she is talking like a Christian, she assures him that she has always been "sereinement incrédule," and adds: "Dieu aurait sans doute besoin des hommes, s'il existait, mais l'homme n'a eu besoin que des hommes pour se guider sur les étoiles" (69). They are thus united in what Fabre-Simmons calls "notre anti-foi, notre paix des profondeurs" (69), but this materialistic "anti-faith" expresses itself a bit differently in Françoise. For her, the meaning of life is to enjoy luxury slowly and peacefully in all its manifestations. She enjoys the life that her husband provides for her and, to occupy fully the hours in her day, she decides to become a *styliste* by opening a high fashion boutique where she will try to create new clothing styles by adapting materials and modes from around the world. In this respect, like Fabre-Simmons, she too reveals herself to be a potentially dynamic person who is prepared to use her wealth in new and innovative ways.

As the novel unfolds, the two main scenes of action are the acquisition of Sangalles's company by Fabre-Simmons and the youthful concerns of the latter's children. There is a third strand that is woven into the fabric of the novel, however, through the relationship between Françoise and her husband's public relations officer, Pierre Mazade. A poet and essayist, Mazade works only half-time for the Fabre-Simmons empire, in order to have the rest of his time free for the creation of his *œuvre*. He is portrayed as being vain and a womanizer, and of course like virtually all the writers in Saint Pierre's novels, he is unmarried, since a commitment to wife and family would limit the time available for his work. Inevitably, he and Françoise are attracted to each other. Then, after several invitations, she agrees to visit Mazade's apartment one afternoon. Once there, however, she realizes that she has gone too far, resists his advances and leaves. But this interlude only serves to rekindle Mazade's ardor. He continues to send her love notes in which he requests another rendezvous and, as one might suspect, one of these notes will be carelessly left in a place where Fabre-Simmons will find it. As he reads it, he is devastated by his wife's infidelity. He has been totally faithful to Françoise and, although he realizes that he has not been as available to his wife and children as much as they would have liked, he is still convinced that he has been a good and generous husband and father: he has used his money to replace the personal attention that he could not give them. Fabre-Simmons does not tell his wife about his discovery, and even when Françoise herself realizes that the letter is gone and that her husband is the only person who could have taken it, he still says nothing. Possessed of enormous will power, he prefers to wait for her initial reaction. As the novel moves rapidly to its climax, all three main elements are still undecided: will maneuvering by a third party keep Fabre-Simmons from gaining a majority interest in Société Sangalles et Fils; will Roland, who has left home and vowed never to return (because his father, angry at the boy's burning of automobiles in a confrontation with police, has set fire to his Triumph, completely destroying it), change his mind and come back to the fold? And, finally, will the close relationship between Fabre-Simmons and his wife dissolve?

In the fast-paced conclusion, Fabre-Simmons does succeed in acquiring Sangalles et Fils and, in the process, relieves Sangalles himself of all responsibility in the new firm. Here, Fabre-Simmons's principal motive is revenge. Since Sangalles had insulted him in the course of the private luncheon that opens the novel and during which Fabre-Simmons had initially proposed a merger, he has been determined not only to acquire Sangalles's company, but also to drive him from power. He has been successful in his design and has created a massive French-owned computer manufacturer capable of facing up to American competition. As for Françoise, he has a detailed discussion with her about Mazade's letter in which she tells him truthfully what has transpired. Without hesitation, Fabre-Simmons fires Mazade to punish him. Finally, Roland confirms in a note that he intends never to return home. His ideal is to engineer a Maoist-style revolution in France, whereas Cécile, who knows where Roland is living, will keep in touch with him while continuing with her studies.

Fabre-Simmons has succeeded in achieving his principal business objectives, but what has he sacrificed in the process? His son Roland is gone, perhaps never to return, and Françoise, despairing of ever seeing very much of her husband, has opened up her boutique to keep herself busy. He has also lost his highly treasured friendship with Pierre Mazade. Earlier he had asked himself, "Tout cet effort, tout ce travail qui n'est pas compris des miens et qui se retourne contre moi, cette fortune et ce tas d'or, cet empire de plus en plus étendu, de plus en plus menacé, tout ça, pour quoi?" (296). Now, alone with his victory, he asks himself the same question. He calls to mind his wife and the "sereine indifférence qu'elle opposait au mystère; ce refus souriant qu'il avait cru longtemps partager— contre laquelle, à présent, il butait" (410). Finally, when he returns home, his house is empty. Roland has run away for good and Cécile is probably out with friends. Françoise will not be coming home until very late. There is only Paul, his gardener, a timid man who usually flees human contact. When Fabre-Simmons asks him if he enjoys his work and is happy in life, Paul thinks for a moment, then nods his head to indicate yes. When Fabre-Simmons presses him to know why, the gardener looks around at the garden and tells him: "Les fleurs, j'y crois" (410).

Thus, as Fabre-Simmons ponders the meaning of life, Saint Pierre seems to be trying to introduce into the novel the nagging question of religious belief. If the essence of what it means to be a Catholic novelist is to present the reader as one's primary concern with the question of a soul's salvation or damnation, this work is probably one of Saint Pierre's least Catholic novels. Although the theological dimension is not absent, it is clearly subordinate to other concerns. And although Fabre-Simmons accomplishes a great deal as a leader in his field—like the creation of new jobs and the advancement of knowledge—he still faces daily the temptation to give himself completely to materialism and materialistic values.

It is worth mentioning that Fabre-Simmons has much in common with other bourgeois fathers who appear in Saint Pierre's fiction. In ignoring his children, he reminds us of the fathers of Marc Van Hussel and of Denis Prullé-Rousseau. The only difference here is one of perspective, for it is the father and not the son who is of principal interest to the narrative voice. Despite his ability to function almost like a god in the world of business, he is still brought back to a human level in his family life. His complaint to Françoise, that his children do not understand and appreciate how important he is in the world of business, underlines Fabre-Simmons's tragic blindness. When he asks Roland why he hates his father so much, the boy responds: "Mais parce que vous ne faites même pas un effort pour nous comprendre" (136), and he is right.

In the end, it is this tragic dimension to Fabre-Simmons's life that strikes us, for he is willing to lose his wife, his children, and his best friend in the name of business success. The diabolical power of materialism, the accumulation of wealth and power as ends in themselves, have led to this empty life, symbolized by an empty home. As Gilbert Ganne so aptly puts it, Saint Pierre's greatest success in this novel is his avoidance of preachiness and a moralizing tone in attacking materialism. He writes: "Son mérite est de nous faire sentir, sans qu'apparaisse chez lui la moindre intention moralisatrice, ce que récèle de vanité tragique ce défi du matérialisme aux valeurs de l'esprit et du cœur."[6] In part for this reason, one is tempted to agree with P. Berthier who called *Le Milliardaire* Saint Pierre's "meilleur livre."[7]

The second novel in what we can call Saint Pierre's Balzacian cycle of novels is *L'Accusée*.[8] Like *Le Milliardaire*, which delineates the relationship between society and a forward-looking businessman, *L'Accusée* recounts the interaction between a woman and the French legal system. Although Carol, the heroine, is a striking individual, her case could be that of any other contemporary French woman. As in the earlier novel, which furnishes an overview of the workings of French industry and its corporate climate, this work gives the reader a comprehensive view of the workings of the legal system.

The story is relatively simple. Carol and Laurent Mansigny have been married for fourteen years and have two children, a twelve year old girl, Dominique, and a boy, Geoffroy, thirteen. Laurent is an officer of a major French bank whose brilliant academic accomplishments and family connections have prepared him for a career that knows no limits. Carol, eleven years younger than Laurent, married him when she was only nineteen. She is from a lower middle-class background and had been studying architecture when she met Laurent and married him six months later. When we meet Carol and the children, she has already left her husband's apartment in the avenue Foch, considered to be one of the better addresses in Paris, to come live temporarily in a friend's apartment that is located in a fictional housing complex called the Cité Montespan. Laurent had driven her out by inviting his personal secretary, an attractive young woman, to come live with them and to sleep in their guest room. Each night, after the children went to bed, he would leave Carol to spend the night with Laetitia, his secretary. Carol, unable to cope with the situation, has simply left the family apartment (which is what Laurent was hoping she would do), but she has also taken the children with her (something he had not anticipated.)

Laurent's goal seems to be to obtain a divorce and at the same time maintain custody of his children. For the past fourteen years, he has enjoyed the company of a string of lovers and has systematically put distance between himself and Carol and all that she loves, including her parents and her sculpture. Thus, more than ever, she clings to her children. He had even gone so far as to introduce her to a friend and colleague, René Damiens, in the hope that he and Carol would become lovers. But he has failed in this design. René and Carol remain friends, however, and in this capacity René stops by from time to time to visit Carol at the Cité Montespan.

Laurent has hired private detectives to watch Carol in the hope that she can be found in a compromising situation with René. As the action of the novel begins, the latter is spending the weekend with Carol and sleeping in the guest room. Suddenly, at 6 a.m. on a Saturday morning, there is a violent knock at the door. Carol asks René to answer the door and when he does two police officers enter quickly and walk throughout the apartment to determine whether the circumstances indicate that Carol might be an adulteress. Under French law at that time, adultery was a criminal act for a woman, whereas for a man it was nothing more than a personal adventure, an escapade. The inspection completed, the officers leave and a few days later Carol receives a warrant ordering her to appear in court.

At the hearing, in which Laurent, through his attorney, Maître Rennenski, seeks to regain custody of the children, Carol exhibits a character trait that will work against her interests throughout the novel. When asked by the judge why she has left her husband, she will not state directly that her husband has taken a series of lovers, culminating in the affair that has literally taken place right in their very home and that has precipitated her departure. Partly out of awe for her husband, his diplomas, his social standing, the fact that he is eleven years her senior and seemingly more mature than she, partly out of concern for her children who, she feels, should be sheltered from knowledge of their father's adventures, and partly out of a natural sense of *pudeur*, a combination of timidity, modesty, and reserve, she feels herself incapable of discussing the most intimate details of her private life in a public courtroom. The judge almost begs her to speak out against her husband, but again, she refuses, going only so far as to say that her husband is morally inadequate to the task of raising two children.

Thus, the court's decision, inevitably, takes the children away from her and sends them back to Laurent.

When Carol begins to realize what has happened, her reaction is a combination of shock and depression. But now it is too late to do anything about the situation. Laurent has invited her to return home, but he has also made it clear that if and when she does, she will be made to pay for what she has done. He seems to want nothing less than to drive her to suicide or to insanity. Under such pressure, she keeps repeating to herself the *leitmotiv* of the novel: "personne n'a moralement le droit d'arracher des enfants à leur mère" (95), and "la femme est placée par la loi en état d'infériorité!" (93). Her only chance to see the children is on weekends. After several weeks, she agrees to have lunch with Laurent at their apartment and to consider returning home. Even though the children are unhappy with their father and are not doing well in school, it will take time for the legal system to get around to this problem. And, of course, Laurent and his attorney know what maneuvers are available to them to slow down the process even further.

Not surprisingly, the centerpiece of the novel and the scene around which the whole work turns is the luncheon scene at their apartment. Laurent has instructed the cook to prepare a magnificent meal and, as in all of Saint Pierre's novels, the act of eating—including the sounds, sights, and sensations associated with it—are copiously and minutely described. The elaborate ceremony of the meal, almost as if it were being staged by a head of state intent on receiving an honored guest, is contrasted with the cruelty of the language that Laurent uses in speaking to his wife. Speaking for herself, Carol admits that the present state of estrangement cannot continue and she seeks an accommodation, although at first she does not go so far as to say that she will actually return. But when she does admit that she is willing to consider this option in order to regain custody of her children, Laurent coldly asserts that when she does come back she will pay dearly for his embarrassment. At this point she caves in and recognizes that he has won: "Est-ce que tu peux avoir pitié de moi?" she asks. "Tu vois, je demande grâce. Tu as gagné" (119). At this point, Laurent, sure of victory, comes around the table, kisses his wife, tells her that the servants have been given the afternoon off and informs her that he expects her to make love with him immediately. Carol refuses and continues to plead her case for getting the children back. As he comes closer, she assures him that she is prepared to go to work to support herself and will not even ask for alimony if she can have the children back. As Laurent begins to lead her towards the bedroom, she pulls a revolver from her handbag and shoots him: first one shot, but then she empties five more bullets into him as he lies dead on the floor. Immediately, she calls the police and waits for them to come and arrest her.

The first part (of three) of the novel ends at this point. The second part will treat Carol's incarceration and the third part will deal with her two-day trial. One cannot help but think of Mauriac's masterpiece, *Thérèse Desqueyroux* (1931), which also deals with the extenuating circumstances of an (attempted) murder of a socially prominent and powerful man by his dominated and little-understood wife. For the most part, however, the resemblances are superficial since Saint Pierre is interested not only in this particular case, with all its psychological and social ramifications, but also in the functioning of France's criminal justice system. For if Carol is first of all a victim of her husband, who has adroitly used the inherently anti-feminine bias of French law to separate her from her children, she subsequently becomes a victim of the system itself.

This second section of the novel details the conditions in which Carol must live for the next sixteen weeks while awaiting trial. In addition to sharing her cell with two other women, one a prostitute and the other a lesbian, she must constantly live with the foul and sickening stench of the prison itself.

> La captive, dans cette alcôve sordide et noyée d'ombre, perçut immédiatement qu'elle y avait une compagne: *l'odeur*. A dire vrai, c'était beaucoup plus qu'une odeur; c'était un foyer de corruption et de relents immondes, exhalés de la cuvette des w.-c., des murs, de cette chose innommable qui devait être un matelas; c'était le chaud parfum des crasses de corps et d'âmes, et des désespoirs, et des haleines de bouches malades; c'était le remugle d'un entassement de misères, qui rayonnait. (179)

Again and again Saint Pierre returns to this theme of human degradation to which criminals are subjected by the system. The prison library is virtually nonexistent and, aside from the obligatory walk in the courtyard each day, there is nothing to do.

Meanwhile, preparations continue for the trial in which Carol will be defended by a young twenty-five year old public defender named Michel Le

Hucheur who, in turn, will persuade his former law professor, the eminent jurist Maître Sénard-Balivière, to advise him on the case. The novel gradually picks up more speed during this second section as Saint Pierre creates an atmosphere of suspense: will Carol be acquitted or not?

In the last part of the novel, a chapter is devoted to each of the two days of the trial, with the turning point, the electrifying *coup de théâtre*, being reserved for the last day. When Lætitia Matelli states firmly to both Le Hucheur and Sénard-Balivière that her relationship with Laurent had not been an intimate one, Carol's prospects seem dim. But slowly, as Le Hucheur succeeds in breaking down her resistance, she admits not only that she had been Laurent's lover for months prior to his death, but also that he had expressly told her that he had wanted her to come live in the family apartment precisely to drive Carol out so that he could be alone with her. But then once Carol left, he also got rid of Lætitia, never to see her again. This testimony sways the jury toward thinking in terms of leniency for Carol. The final vote, when it comes, is seven to five, the majority being of the opinion that Carol's act had been premeditated. But since a majority of two-thirds is necessary for a conviction, she receives only a five-year suspended sentence and is set free. There is irony in the verdict, of course, since the majority of the members of the jury think that she is guilty despite the circumstances. Enough of them, however, deem her act to be one that was committed on the spur of the moment to absolve her from the charge of first degree murder.

One of Saint Pierre's main concerns in this novel is France's Napoleonic Code which, despite revisions, is still the law of the land. If a woman can be jailed for adultery, whereas no penalty is prescribed for an adulterous male, then something is wrong with the law. From the moment when Carol loses custody of her children because her husband has hired a skilled lawyer who knows how to use the law to Laurent's advantage, to the end of the trial, Saint Pierre paints a picture of a legal system, reinforced by a traditional power system, in which men reign supreme. Even Judge Thirel, who hears Carol's case, recognizes how the system works against women: "Elle est jeune et belle, ma meurtrière," he confides to his associate Saint-Galaix. "Elle méritait peut-être mieux que notre 'justice'—que cette espèce d'idole momifiée, impotente et stérile . . ." (271-72).

Maître Saint-Galaix, the presiding judge in the Paris area, is a practicing and convinced Catholic who, because of his faith and his thirst for justice, is quietly laboring to reform the criminal justice system.

Significantly, Saint-Galaix is presented neither as a saint nor as a hero, but simply as a Christian witness attempting to implement the teachings of the gospel in daily life. During a pretrial interview with Carol, he asks her if she believes in God. When she says no, he responds "c'est dommage" (173), and asks his secretary to strike both the question and the answer from the transcript of the interview. Perhaps partly as a result of this question, Carol finds herself, during her incarceration, wondering more and more about God's existence, but she reaches no final conclusions. The fact that she is even asking herself such a question, however, seems to indicate the initial stirrings of grace within her.

The alert reader who knows nothing of Michel de Saint Pierre's personal orthodoxy could probably guess that this novel was written by a man of faith because of the half dozen or so times in which the question of the existence of God comes up. Beyond this, however, there are no direct allusions to religion so that the book, in its obvious zeal to argue for justice and fairness in society, might just as well have been written by an agnostic humanist as by a Christian. But Saint Pierre seems to want it this way, for the society in which he, as a Christian, finds himself, is one that has become almost completely desacralized. With its chief weapons of money and connections, the bourgeois oligarchy that rules France largely for its own benefit, has few spiritual second thoughts about its behavior. Without pity, but with the clear eye of an objective Balzacian narrator, Saint Pierre shows the extent to which sexual equality and true compassion are missing from the societal structure.

As in the other novels beginning with *Le Milliardaire*, Saint Pierre is attempting to show us the lies and injustices that we tolerate. He is trying to speak out on behalf of innocent victims. Modern democratic society, despite its proclaimed good intentions, is still guilty of oversights. There are people, innocent victims, who are not caught by the safety net and who fall between the cracks. Carol is one such person.

That he chose a female protagonist and wrote a novel that a feminist would have to smile upon, is all the more striking in that female characters usually play only a secondary role in his fiction. As a general rule, they are not as fully developed as their male counterparts, with the exception of Jeanne and Daisy in *Les Aristocrates*. In fact, one might argue that the subject of *L'Accusée* is as much the legal condition of women in France as it is a protest against the legal and penal systems themselves. By virtue of the fact that Carol would have had no problem whatsoever with the law if she had been a man and not a woman, this conclusion is inescapable.

L'Accusée was a significant popular success which was later the subject of a well-received French television adaptation. This fact once again confirms that Saint Pierre usually succeeded in meeting his primary objective as a novelist: to be read and understood by ordinary people, *les honnêtes gens*, who can thereby profit from both the esthetic pleasure of a well-told story and the moral message embedded within.

Jacques Vier's reaction to the novel furnishes an excellent example of the importance of Saint Pierre's popular success, which, then as now, went against the prevailing fashion in intellectual circles. Vier begins by praising Saint Pierre for his obvious virtues:

> Michel de Saint Pierre connaît à fond son métier de romancier et ne perd pas son temps en recherches inutiles sur la création littéraire. Il sait conter une histoire aux rebondissements pathétiques, qui permettent aux caractères de s'affirmer et d'illustrer des cas de conscience en rapport avec l'actualité.

But this praise is intensified when we recall what Saint Pierre does *not* do in his books. Vier goes on:

> Je ne cesserai pas de m'en prendre à tous les archi-cuistres de l'esthé-tique, qui profitent de colloques universitaires pour enseigner, selon les lois bouffonnes de je ne sais quel structuralisme ou de je ne sais quelle sémiologie, leur métier aux écrivains créateurs, alors qu'ils n'ont jamais été capables, pour leur compte, d'aligner quatre vers sur l'aurore, le crépuscule, ou sur les yeux de leur Dulcinée, ni de raconter comment la marquise sortit à cinq heures afin de retrouver un galant dans un salon de thé.[9]

This quote is helpful in enabling us to understand that Saint Pierre's audience is not high brow and intellectually oriented, but middle brow and down to earth. While intellectual fads in Paris changed from the existentialism that prevailed in the late forties when he was beginning his career as a novelist, through succeeding trends like structuralism, post-structuralism and semiology, Saint Pierre remained faithful to his own vision of what the novel should be. That vision, less pretentious, but no less important than the reigning fashions, seeks to create a work that one can understand and interpret without the intermediation of a critic. Christine Arnothy confirms the effect on her of Saint Pierre's accomplished style: "... l'art et le talent de Michel de Saint Pierre consistent à faire accepter, et apprécier même, la sottise du personnage. *L'Accusée* est un roman parfois tendre, souvent violent, de temps à autre agaçant ... Le livre se lit, en tout cas, sans qu'on ait envie de l'abandonner en cours de route."[10]

The resounding success of Saint Pierre's new direction was commented on in *Etudes* by P. Berthier: "Aujourd'hui, c'est pour la promotion des droits de la femme que se bat Michel de Saint Pierre: sa fougue parfois emportée, sa générosité au service de la justice, qui ne vont pas sans un brin de manichéisme, retrouvent ici la réussite vigoureuse du *Milliardaire*."[11] With two solid successes behind him in which he attempted to analyze contemporary social problems, he would try in his next novel to write a "roman-chronique" that would bear witness on behalf of Israël and Zionism.

7. The Catholic Novel Revisited

THE LONG TITLE OF *JE REVIENDRAI SUR LES AILES DE L'AIGLE*[1] IS taken from the prophet Zacharia and refers to an apocalyptic time when all Jews will be reassembled from all the corners of the earth to dwell forever in their promised land. Since the novel covers the 1934-76 time period and focuses the reader's attention on the sufferings of Jews at the hands of the Nazis and their cohorts, the founding of the state of Israel and the wars that took place in 1948, 1954, and 1967, the title is well chosen. In fact the novel reads much like a chronicle (albeit a biased one that is heavily weighted in favor of the Jews to the disadvantage of the Palestinians), but since the term "novel" in our century has been expanded to incorporate just about every conceivable type of fiction, even "historical fiction," that is, a fictional tale woven around historical events and incorporating historical documents, we must be content to call this work a novel. As a novel, however, it does not succeed very well, for the reader finds it difficult to overlook the fact that everything is being arranged here by the author to support his thesis: that the foundation of Israel is the result of a "promesse divine." For this reason, the book argues, Christians and Arabs, as well as Jews, should support its existence.

Although this work fails as a novel, it is more successful as a political and religious pamphlet. No matter what the reader's opinions and beliefs might be regarding Israel and the relationship between Christianity and Judaism, one cannot remain indifferent to this book. From the opening chapter, set in a private, Catholic secondary school classroom in which the religious teacher, le père Rutebeuf and his students discuss the meaning of Holy Week, to the final scenes of the 1967 Six Day War, the novel is gripping as a work of politics and history written from a very definite point of view.

Jean-Louis Ezine, commenting on *Je reviendrai sur les ailes de l'aigle* in *Les Nouvelles Littéraires* asserts that "Israël est le personnage principal"[2] of the work. Although the novel does have traditional characters, it is nonetheless true that this is a thesis novel or a political novel more than a novel of manners. Its thesis is simple: the Jews have been so persecuted for the past 2,000 years, a persecution that culminates in the Nazi era, that they deserve a homeland of their own. To defend and support this thesis, Saint Pierre chronicles the friendship of two Frenchmen from their teenage years through World War II, the creation of the state of Israel, the Nuremburg trials, and the wars of 1948, 1954, and 1967.

The thought often comes to mind, in reading this novel, that Saint Pierre might just as easily have treated the same theme in the form of a historical study, but he chose the novel form instead for the following reason: "J'aurais pu faire un ouvrage d'histoire sur Israël, car je connais bien l'âme juive et l'angoisse de ce peuple qui ne sait plus très bien s'il est élu ou maudit. Mais dans un roman, je peux montrer les Juifs en action avec leurs qualités et leurs défauts."[3] This quote is rather typical of Saint Pierre and of his lack of concern for sensitive ears. For even though this novel is solidly pro-Israel and adamantly anti-Arab from a political point of view, it still manages, from a religious point of view, to make a number of serious criticisms of the Jewish state.

Since this was Saint Pierre's first novel since *L'Accusée* (1972), which had sold over 200,000 copies and been made into a French television movie, the public was ready again to respond to his work and did so. *Je reviendrai* became an immediate best-seller and, at the same time, provoked a great deal of controversy. After all, here was a celebrated Catholic writer whose name had been associated for the past decade with the defense of traditional Catholicism and a rejection of many of the reforms of Vatican II, supporting Jews and Israel. But Saint Pierre claims to have seen no contradiction at all in his position on this matter. Talking with Gilbert Ganne of the daily *L'Aurore*, he stated his belief that "pour les Juifs, le Messie doit venir; pour les chrétiens, il doit revenir; mais c'est le même en définitive que nous attendons les uns et les autres."[4] He attempts here to keep to a primarily religious viewpoint with regard to Israel, for he sees Jews in that country as a group fulfilling a divine promise to reoccupy the promised land, whereas Jews in France are simply individuals like all other citizens and as such are not necessarily members of a nefarious or privileged people.

The opening chapter of *Je reviendrai* is gripping in that it treats the eternal problem of anti-Semitism in France, especially among traditional bourgeois Catholics. The chapter derives extra force from the fact that the setting is a Catholic secondary school in Versailles, in other words, a fictionalized version of the school, Saint Jean-de-Béthune, that Saint Pierre himself attended as a boy. Thus, not only is the scene one that the author has already experienced in one form or another, it is also one that enables him to deal with characters that he treats with great sympathy, understanding, and power: adolescents.

It is Holy Week, April 1934. Le père Rutebeuf, teaching a catechism class to seventeen-year-olds, takes up the question of the responsibility for Christ's death. The point that he is trying to make is that all men and women, even those in Versailles in 1934, are somehow responsible. The students take turns reading from St. Luke's account of Christ's passion and death. But a student who has learned at home to hate Jews, asks permission to read from St. Matthew's account of the same events, an account in which we find the famous quotation: "Let his blood be on us and on our children" (Matt. 27 : 26). Rutebeuf lets him make this point, but then responds by quoting Luke again, as follows: "Jésus était suivi d'une grande foule de peuple, et de femmes qui se frappaient la poitrine et qui se lamentaient pour lui" (26). His conclusion is that there were two groups of Jews taking positions on either side of the question of Jesus' identity at the time of the crucifixion. Thus, then as now, there were two crowds, one proclaiming the innocence of Jesus and the other rejecting him. To Rutebeuf, there can only be one conclusion:

> Alors, voudriez-vous que je ne sais combien de millions d'hommes, pendant deux mille ans, et bien au-delà peut-être, soient maudits sans espoir malgré la bonté de Dieu, parce qu'un jour une foule excitée a fait ce que font toutes les foules depuis le commencement du monde? (26-27)

Saint Pierre heightens the tension in the class by including in it a converted Jew, Michel Cohen, who feels personally attacked when Jews are presented as the murderers of Jesus. Cohen has converted all by himself, even over the objections of his parents who, because of their "respect absolu de la liberté des autres" (60), not only have tolerated this decision but are presumably paying for the boy's education as a boarding student far from their home in Lyons. Michel's best friend is Bruno Martinville, referred to a number of times in the novel as a "descendant des Vikings," which for Saint Pierre means that he is an authentic Norman. Their friendship, from 1934 through the next thirty years, will be the means through which the author will tell the story of Israel and how he views the ideology of Zionism during this time period. But to return to this opening scene of the novel, Rutebeuf terminates his discussion of the problem of assigning guilt for the death of Jesus—even though he has virtually no chance of changing the mind of the student who raised the objection in the first place—by engaging in an exegesis of the eleventh chapter of Paul's *Epistle to the Romans*, which deals specifically with this whole question. Paul's conclusion is that "as the chosen people, they are still loved by God, loved for the sake of their ancestors. God never takes back his gifts or revokes his choice" (Rom. 10 : 28-29). With St. Paul, le père Rutebeuf also concludes that all mankind, every individual, is responsible in part for Jesus' death, and not the Jews alone as a race. This is obviously anything but a trivial subject to treat at the outset of a novel, and the direct manner in which Saint Pierre approaches it, recognizing honestly and openly that dislike, even hatred, of Jews has existed, and at times flourished, in France's Catholic schools over the years, makes for powerful, emotional reading.

Finally, in the conclusion to this opening chapter, Michel Cohen challenges the Jew-baiter to a fist fight over this issue and his friend, Martinville, backs him up. Thus, the stage is set for the depiction of a friendship that will last from Hitler's rise to power until the June War of 1967.

Succeeding chapters follow what we know to be some of the major stages in Saint Pierre's life. We see Michel and Bruno as sailors together in the French Navy in 1939 and then, during the Occupation, as members of a clandestine network of *résistants* in Paris. At war's end, Bruno becomes a journalist and remains a confirmed bachelor. After the years of excitement and adventure, he feels like a fish out of water. His life has no clear-cut goals. Thus, to fill his free time, he chases women. Michel, on the other hand, has become a lawyer and is happily married to an orthodox Jewish wife, Ilana. They have a son, Itamar, and they also welcome into their home Michel's youngest sister, Miriam, who was only three years old when the war ended and who is the only other survivor in Michel's family.

Bruno, as a journalist, will cover the Nuremburg trials, the 1948 Israeli-Arab war, and the capture and return of Eichmann to Israel in 1961. Finally, from France he will follow the events of the Six Day War of 1967. During each of these major events and periods of crisis, Ilana, as an orthodox Jew and dedicated Zionist, wants desperately to separate Michel from his allegiance to Jesus. Repeatedly, the narrator contrasts their position on burning political and religious issues in order to make clear what he takes to be the difference between Judaism and Christianity.

During the Nuremburg trials, for instance, Ilana wants all the captured Nazis hanged to pay for their treatment of the Jews. Interestingly, Martinville, the authentic descendent of the Vikings, feels the same way. Michel, however, believes in a God of justice and love. Thus, while he is willing to concede that justice has been done at Nuremburg, he has grave doubts about the morality of the whole undertaking. His concern is two-fold. First, the trials seem to him to be primarily a version of justice meted out by conquerers for the simple reason that the Nazi defense lawyers had repeatedly been kept from asking questions about other atrocities, like the massive bombing of German cities, the use of the atomic bomb, the murder, rape, and plunder that occurred everywhere that Soviet soldiers went, and the slaughter of uncounted thousands of German prisoners at Stalingrad, among others. His second concern is about the lack of love and compassion in the trials. Since he believes in a God of love, he can only be disappointed here. As he puts it, at Nuremburg "on courrait après la justice, mais l'amour n'y trouvait pas son compte" (103).

The next crisis that brings the two friends together is Israel's 1948 war of independence. Michel's wife, Ilana, is staunchly Zionist and would some day like to raise her two children, Myriam and Itamar, in the land of her ancestors. By means of cable dispatches sent back to Martinville's office and through newspaper headlines read by the Cohens, the reader learns of the activities of the Israeli army and of the terrorist groups Irgun and Stern, lead respectively by Menachem Begin and Itzak Shamir. Martinville, very much like Saint Pierre, supports all such activities since he considers them to be essentially defensive in nature against the overwhelming numerical superiority of the Arabs. In the meantime, Ilana has continued her Torah studies with Rabbi Grüner who, like her, warmly supports Zionist ideology. To him, though, Judaism is basically a religion and not a race, and for this reason he sees Israel's salvation as being contingent upon a solid religious foundation. Without this foundation, it imperils its very existence. Among his collected writings, Ilana comes across the following:

> Certains Juifs pensent que si la pratique de l'antique religion d'Israël
> l'empêche d'accéder à ce qu'on appelle "la société moderne," eh bien,
> mieux vaut y renoncer. Les temps nouveaux leur paraissent incompa-
> tibles avec la vénérable tradition religieuse. Ils la détruisent sans
> broncher. Ils briseraient en souriant les tables de la Loi. Moi, je vous
> dis qu'un Israël rationaliste et laïc perdrait l'essence même de sa force.
> La religion d'Israël, c'est la chevelure de Samson. (141-42)

Rabbi Grüner, inevitably, becomes a disruptive force in the Cohen marriage since, in his eyes, Ilana's husband, born a Jew but converted to Christianity, is an idolator. Ilana regularly reproaches her husband for wanting to convert her and insists that he revert to the religion of his ancestors, but he refuses. Instead, he proposes a common ground that they can share. He tries to present Jesus as a Jew who has studied the scriptures very closely. The New Testament, he pleads, is only a restatement of the quest for justice initially expressed in the Old Testament. Finally, he tells her, they both live in anticipation of the same thing: ". . . pour elle, le Messie doit venir; pour moi, il doit revenir. . . . c'est finalement le même, l'un et l'autre, que nous attendons" (147).

The next major events are the war over the Suez Canal in 1954 and the Eichmann affair in 1960-61. During this period, Martinville gets permission to write a series of articles on Israel for his newspaper. He is convinced that a wave of irreligion has passed over the Western world since the sixteenth century, but that the creation of the State of Israel is perhaps a sign that this trend will now be reversed. As he tells his editor, the skeptic Jamieski:

> Or Dieu—il l'a dit si bien et si souvent—veut que son peuple élu se
> rassemble en Israël et qu'il y reste. Pourquoi? Parce qu'Israël, en
> tâtonnant, malgré ses erreurs et ses fautes, est restée à portee de Dieu.
> Israël, c'est la présence divine manifestée au milieu des nations établies,
> des nations furieuses, c'est le peuple de la Bible revenant dans le désert
> des âmes. . . . (154-55)

This statement does much to illuminate the major theme of the novel, except for one last element that Martinville states explicitly: "selon moi, tout gouvernement d'Israël qui ne croit pas expressément en Dieu est illégitime" (155). But when Jamieski retorts that it is well known that David Ben Gurion, the first president of Israel, is an agnostic, Martinville vows to put this question directly to Ben Gurion. When he does so, on a subsequent trip to Israël, Ben Gurion tells him that he, like his father, is a free thinker who does not believe in God, but he adds that religious belief is not necessary to be a good Jew: "Ce que je dis, c'est qu'un bon Juif ne peut pas ignorer la Torah! Nous avons vécu, mon père et moi, selon les prescriptions religieuses du Judaïsme et je connais mes prophètes aussi bien qu'un rabbin!" (200). The conflict generated by these two divergent views of Israel's nature will be repeated again and again through statements of various characters during the rest of the novel and into the epilogue, dated July 1967, after the resounding Israeli victories in June of that year. But Martinville is surely speaking for Saint Pierre when he states that if Israel loses sight of its "mission prophétique" (362), the people of the Bible will risk facing exile once more.

Also by novel's end, Michel and Ilana will have moved to Jerusalem and intend to live the rest of their lives there. During the 1967 war, their son Itamar loses his hand and their daughter Myriam returns from Paris to live in Jerusalem where she feels that she henceforth belongs. Finally, the Cohens have a new child, a son named Nathanaël, who is born in Israel.

Unfortunately, by this time neither the Cohens nor Martinville, the author's *porte-parole*, have very much credibility left as characters, for they have devolved into what can be called merely useful tools in Saint Pierre's hands to defend his thesis that all Frenchmen should support Israel, whose creation is in the process of fulfilling biblical prophecies. Enemies of Israel, whatever their motivation or point of view, are simply enemies of God. The Arabs, guilty of creating the refugee problem and of not attempting to solve it, cannot be trusted. Any treaty that they might ever sign means nothing, for they are merely "chiffons de papier n'engageant pas leur ombrageux honneur" (164). The United Nations? It is nothing less than a propaganda outlet used by the Arabs, a "vide absolu" (359).

But Saint Pierre's main concern here seems to be the commitment to Israel of his readers in France. As a familiar name on the traditional right wing in France, a group in which dislike and suspicion of Jews are widespread, he surprised many people by writing this book, especially since France in 1967 had abruptly changed sides in the Middle East by stopping the sale of any more arms to Israel and becoming both an arms supplier and a moral supporter of the Arab cause. The reaction of the French extreme right, traditionally committed to anti-Semitism, is clearly expressed by Michel Fromentoux, who reviewed the novel in the Maurrasian weekly *Aspects de la France*.[5] He grants Saint Pierre's argument that hatred of Jews is unjustified and incompatible with true Christianity. He calls this kind of mindless racial hatred "antisémitisme de peau" and condemns it. But then he invokes every Frenchman's right to practice "antisémitisme d'Etat," which is justified as long as Jews, as a group, 1) do not convert to Christianity and thereby recognize that the Messiah has already come, 2) continue to have a deeper commitment to Israel than to the countries in which they live and, 3) persist in attempting to foment revolution around the world. This type of anti-Semitism, says Fromentoux, is a "réflexe de légitime défense" (17), and he chides Saint Pierre for not bringing it out in the novel. This review is an important one in that it enables us to distance Saint Pierre, often condemned by writers and intellectuals of the left because of his traditionalist views, from the truly anti-Republican and racist right in France. A book like this could not have been written by someone who shares their blind and virulent hatred of Jews.

Pierre Fritsch aptly calls the novel a "roman-chronique" in which "certaines pages sont plus de l'ordre du compte-rendu historique que de celui du roman,"[6] and this observation brings us to the major strengths and weaknesses of the work. To put it simply, the book never really succeeds as a novel, for its characters never cease to be mere excuses for the author to present his thesis. As a historico-political text, however, the book is quite successful and, given the situation in which it was written, that is, with both the Giscard government and the majority of Frenchmen more sympathetic to the Palestinians than to the Israelis, one might even call it daring, a political act of courage.

On balance, one might be tempted to reject *Je reviendrai* as merely a manifestation of Zionist propaganda, were it not for the name of the author. For the novel is nothing less than a call to all Frenchmen, but especially to traditional French Catholics, to support Israel. It stresses the spiritual ties that link Jews and Christians and argues that the Messiah that the Jews await is the same person, Jesus, whose second coming is awaited by Christians. Through Rabbi Grüner, he tries to make a case for the idea that what he calls the "âme juive" is essentially religious and not ethnic, sociological, or financial in nature. Any Jewish supporter of Israel can read this novel as a political blank check in support of that country, except for one point: the need for Israel to continue to be a nation with a fundamentally religious character that is inhabited by and ruled over by people who believe in God. Since Saint Pierre's argument rests on the legitimacy of Jewish prophecies foretelling the return of the Jews to the Promised Land, he logically concludes that the country established and justified by the scriptures cannot be secular and materialistic in nature. If it is, he warns, it risks being annihilated and its inhabitants dispersed once again. Of course there are many Jews, although a numerical minority, who cling to the idea that Israel must have a distinct religious character marked by outward and formalized ritual, like strict observance of the Sabbath. Most Israelis, however, disagree with this point of view and would prefer to see their country become more secularized, on the American model, with the strength of the religious parties reduced accordingly. But this is a risky course, warns Saint Pierre, because for Israel, "sa religion, c'est la chevelure de Samson."

Putting his ideas in slightly different language, the author has Michel express the danger facing Israel as double in nature: "levantinisation," that is, engaging in underhanded and illicit dealings and "américanisation" (362), which is defined as becoming "le lieu des grands hôtels sans âme, du chewing-gum, des majorettes et des serpentins, de l'efficacité matérialiste, du réfrigérateur et de la télévision, de la valeur-dollar érigée en valeur spirituelle, et de l'ennui" (362). All these values are not only seen as essentially evil by Saint Pierre, but are also associated specifically with the United States. Obviously, the case is overstated here, for why cannot Israelis aspire to legitimate creature comforts, just as so many Europeans, including Frenchmen, do? The answer is that Saint Pierre sees Israel's existence as an essentially religious phenomenon. Thus, all the dietary and travel restrictions that the orthodox Jews of Israel seek to impose on the nonreligious majority of cultural Jews seem to be supported by Saint Pierre. Michel sums up his misgivings about the future when he says: "Or nous sommes entrés, tu le sais bien, dans l'ère messianique. Et je redoute pour Israël tous ces gouvernants mâles et femelles qui ne croient pas en Dieu" (350).

Michel de Saint Pierre spent several months living in Israel to document this novel. He spoke with leaders of all tendencies and factions, including Arab members of the Knesset. He also visited Palestinian refugee camps and concludes that their existence is the fault of the Arabs, not the Jews. For if, he argues, at the time of gaining its independence, Israel could take in 800,000 Jewish refugees from Arab lands, the Arabs should have been able to take in the Palestinians. Although the Arabs are recognized as essentially good people and as courageous fighters, they are also portrayed as victims of hateful leaders motivated by their own abomination of Jews. Jewish military and political leaders, on the other hand, are presented as sensitive, well-educated, and intelligent people who seek only one thing: peace with secure borders.

Finally, the other complicating factor in a novel that is otherwise sympathetic to Judaism and supportive of Zionist ideology is the introduction of a Christian into a Jewish household. When interviewed by the popular daily *France-Soir* about this novel, Saint Pierre stated that he had never received so many letters in reaction to a book. When asked about the reaction of his Jewish readers, he answered:

> Tout ce qui touche Israël les enchante. Mais ils n'apprécient pas l'intrusion de Jésus dans une famille juive, parce que, disent-ils "ça complique les choses." Pour moi, Israël, c'est le pays d'Abraham, de Moïse, de David, de Salomon, mais aussi celui de Jésus, de sa mère et des apôtres. Si je n'en avais pas tenu compte, j'aurais complètement escamoté mon sujet.[7]

The reasons for Michel Cohen's conversion, which has taken place before the action of the novel begins, are never described in detail. We know only that he had read the gospels as a boy and converted as a personal reaction to this experience. But this is really not sufficient to enable us to understand why he is such a Christian idealist, forever pardoning his enemies and understanding his adversaries' point of view. One wonders how his marriage to Ilana, who keeps a kosher household, studies the Torah incessantly, and devotes her spare time to hunting for Nazis, can possibly endure. But this contradiction is perhaps better understood not so much on the representational level of the characters themselves, but as a symbol of the complex relationship between Jews and Christians. Sharing to a large degree the same traditions, with a common reverence for the same holy books, they nonetheless differ strongly on a number of basic points. It is this state of creative tension that Saint Pierre attempts to evoke—with mixed results—in this ambitious "roman-chronique."

Je reviendrai is an excellent example of how difficult it can be to clearly distinguish between Saint Pierre as a Catholic novelist and as a witness to his age. Whereas the latter tendency had predominated in *Le*

Milliardaire and *L'Accusée*—and would again in *Docteur Erikson* (1982) and *Le Double Crime de l'impasse Salomon* (1984)—this book leans in both directions. Probably inspired in part by Saint Pierre's extensive knowledge of Léon Bloy's work, often obsessed as it is with the Catholic view of the redemptive role accorded to Jews in the divine plan of salvation, this book never really decides what it wants to be. Although it ultimately fails as a novel, this setback is compensated for by its sincerity and conviction as a gesture of friendship toward French Jews.

As we have already seen, the opening pages of a Saint Pierre novel often contain a key for understanding the rest of the work. The long description of the family château in *Les Aristocrates* and the detailed evocation of the cemetery overlooking Villedieu in *Les Nouveaux Prêtres* are evident examples. The castle that the Marquis de Maubrun is willing to make enormous sacrifices to maintain is a living symbol of his caste, just as the cemetery represents the living dead of certain de-Christianized working-class Paris suburbs. In *La Passion de l'abbé Delance*,[8] which is a sequel to *Les Nouveaux Prêtres* that attempts to bring us up to date on the state of the parish fifteen years after the end of the action described in the earlier novel, the opening pages describe the Saint-Marc parish church in Villedieu:

> L'église paroissiale à Saint-Marc de Villedieu, dans la banlieue de Paris, menaçait ruine.
>
> C'était un vénérable sanctuaire du XIIIe siècle, sommé d'un clocher en flèche dont la coiffe d'ardoise bleue s'ajustait avec des coquetteries féminines. Les arcs-boutants moussus, la dentelle des fenestrages, une nef élevée lui composaient cette silhouette irremplaçable des églises qui recouvrirent la France d'un blanc manteau, à la meilleure époque du style gothique. Maison de Dieu, elle exigeait un respect débordant d'amour. A l'intérieur du sanctuaire, les piliers, les ogives, la grande coquille de nef envahie d'ombre et de silence, une acoustique dont les secrets sont depuis longtemps perdus, les prières accumulées depuis des siècles sous les vieilles pierres extasiées, tout appelait à la contemplation divine. Une cantate de Bach, un oratorio de Haendel y trouvaient leur place avec d'étranges exactitudes. Et la masse obscure du peuple de Dieu se sentait à l'aise dans l'église paroissiale de Saint-Marc, où la foi des petites âmes clignotait avec la lumière des cierges. Il y avait

encore, au fond du chœur patiné d'encens et d'oraison, un maître-autel du XVIIIe siècle, qui ne servait plus depuis le Concile, mais que veillait, elargi jusqu à la voûte, un grand soleil de bois doré. (17-18)

The church is a living repository of the collective memory and presence of the local parishioners over a period of seven centuries. It stands for tradition, for Catholic, pre-revolutionary, and monarchical France. The inspirational and uplifting nature of the edifice is evident from the fact that great musical works or magnificent wood carvings from other ages naturally blend in with the church's atmosphere. In addition, Saint-Marc offers concrete and eloquent testimony to the faith of the thousands of believers who, over the centuries, have sacrificed and worked together to preserve the building for the present generation of parishioners. That faith is reflected in the flicker of the devotional candles. But now, due to changes in the nature of the local population, its elected leaders and, perhaps, most importantly, the local bishop himself, the church has been allowed to deteriorate and will soon be destroyed.

The reason for the state of neglect in which the church finds itself is that Jules Barré, a curate in *Les Nouveaux Prêtres*, but now the regional bishop for the area in which Villedieu is located, has decided that the church is simply an old building which, because it stands quite a distance from the recently built apartment complexes in which most of Villedieu's population is housed, has "perdu sa vocation urbaine" (18). Its architecture, outmoded and impractical, is no longer appropriate for the "formes modernes du culte" (18). Barré, in cooperation with the local government, which by law is required to pay for the upkeep of the church, has decided that it should be allowed to fall apart so that it can be torn down that much sooner. They have also been careful not to register it as a historical landmark—a step that could be easily taken—in order to hasten its demise. Saint-Marc's magnificent stained glass windows have been registered with the state and they will be preserved, but everything else must go.

It has been fifteen years since our last visit to Saint-Marc Parish. We learn right away in the opening pages of the novel that Paul Delance fell ill shortly after the end of the action described in *Les Nouveaux Prêtres* and that for most of the past fifteen years he has struggled to overcome tuberculosis. Like his father who died of the same illness—caused by his work in a cement factory—Paul had been afraid that he too would succumb to it. But he has fought back and won. Healed, his main desire was to begin again in parish work and his old friend, Mgr. Merignac, now cardinal archbishop of Paris, has granted his wish. He will return as pastor at Saint-Marc.

Saint Pierre's narrative voice in *La Passion de l'abbé Delance* is considerably more caustic toward Barré than it had been in *Les Nouveaux Prêtres*. Here, in the paragraph that brings the reader up to date on his career over the past fifteen years, he is described as an extreme version of a post-conciliar priest. His principal attributes are that he: 1) is "armé de théories sociales aggressives," 2) is willing to work with Communists, 3) is infatuated with novelty, 4) condemns the "Eglise-institution" of which he is a part, 5) overlooks church history prior to Vatican II when it suits his purposes to do so, and 6) interprets the meaning of the Council itself in a selective way, taking what coincides with his views and rejecting the rest. His ultimate goals in behaving this way are to adapt the church and its teachings to the modern world, make the gospel intelligible to secularists, bring man closer to God by serving his temporal needs and, finally, simplify doctrine and streamline dogma in order to make them acceptable to the greatest number of people, thereby promoting Christian unity.

The struggle between Jules Barré, who has been fighting actively for his ideas during the past fifteen years, and Paul Delance, who has been held back from an active life because of his illness, is more extreme here than in *Les Nouveaux Prêtres*. In part because of the limitations imposed on his life by sickness, but also because of his personal temperament, Delance has given himself over to a life of prayer and meditation and has "affiné sa vie intérieure, jusqu'à vivre dans un perpétuel contact divin" (21). He has read extensively in Saint Theresa of Lisieux and Saint Francis de Sales. Like St. John of the Cross, whose mystical writings he has also absorbed, he has experienced "la conversation fréquente avec Dieu," and "de longues méditations qui l'isolent totalement du monde" (21). In a word, Delance is a traditional pre-conciliar priest who is attempting to develop his spiritual life in the classical manner, through prayer and penance. He presumes that if he is successful in cultivating his inner life, all else will follow naturally.

The two extreme points of view represented by these two priests are brought together early in the novel. The technique employed is reminiscent of that used at the end of *Les Nouveaux Prêtres*. In that novel, we recall that in order to illustrate the attitudinal differences between Delance and the "prêtres progressistes" of the "red belt," Paul had expressed his conservative views at a meeting of priests from the local area, a meeting in which he alone represented a traditional, some would say arch-conservative, point of view. Here Saint Pierre uses the same technique to show that prevailing Catholic attitudes have moved to the left and in the process shifted someone like Paul Delance farther to the right than he had seemed to be fifteen years earlier.

It is a dark and cold November day and we are on the fifth floor of a rather dingy public housing project. The local Communist mayor, who controls access to such places in Villedieu, has agreed to let Saint-Marc Parish use this large, public room as a "lieu de culte" (24). As part of their agreement, the old church will be demolished, thereby saving the municipality quite a bit of money. In attendance at the meeting, in addition to Paul (who has only been in his new functions for one day, and has barely had the opportunity to get to know his two curates, Lucien Cornelli and Jean-Pierre Leblanc), are three architects, the mayor, regional bishop Mgr. Jules Barré and assorted journalists from post-conciliar Catholic publica-ions with preposterous names like *Salut, les Chrétiens* and *Hello Jésus*. There is also one from *Messager Chrétien*, the latter a thinly veiled reference to *Témoignage Chrétien*, which had attacked *Les Nouveaux Prêtres* so vehemently.

Mgr. Barré is dressed in civil attire, giving no hint of his ecclesias-tical status, and he listens approvingly as one of the architects, Le Récamier, talks of the need to dismantle the parish church. Since the new apartment complexes have been built in another part of town, the church is now incon-veniently located for most people. In addition, it is expensive to maintain. Also, since it is a vestige of the Middle Ages, he considers it to be a reminder of the past for those Catholics with a "mentalité médiévale" who cannot accept "le devenir de l'histoire" (23). Finally, he tells his listeners that the "âge sacral" has been replaced by an "âge technique" and that the age of the "église-monument" and "église-institution" is dead and buried. Thus, in a new liturgical age, this outdated structure has lost its reason for being and ought to be demolished. One sentence aptly sums up his re-marks: "Allons! Plus de médiévalisme, plus d'anachronisme . . ." (25). As a replacement for the church, he proposes the large room in which they are seated. Located on the fifth floor of a massive apartment building, it is what he calls a "lieu plurifonctionnel" which can be used for any number of purposes, including liturgy. With a sliding door, it can be divided into two separate rooms and its furniture is also adaptable to many uses. His conclusion is that this space can serve as an ideal "centre polymorphe" (27) where Catholics can gather to "reprendre haleine, clarifier nos motivations, chercher le recul nécessaire pour juger nos attitudes et pour nous remettre en question" (27). Ironically, he makes no mention of prayer.

It is obvious to Paul Delance that everyone else in the room is in agreement with what Le Récamier has said. Leblanc and Cornelli, his young curates, are enthusiastic because a room like this will help priests to prepare for the day when there will be few clerics left and the church on the local level will be predominently in the hands of laymen. They feel more at home in a space like this because a monumental church in the style of Saint-Marc only brings back memories of the old church, the one that claimed to possess a monopoly on truth. "J'ai accepté de m'embarquer dans une église qui n'a plus de certitude, qui essaye honnêtement de trouver sa voie parmi les hommes, et qui ne pense pas avoir le monopole de la vérité" (29-30), says Leblanc. To which Cornelli responds:

> Les certitudes orgueilleuses, c'est fini!! Ce qu'on veut, nous autres, c'est rejoindre l'homme, c'est trouver l'homme par le moyen de l'Evangile. Si les bourgeois dorés sur tranche et les militaires retraités de Villedieu n'aiment pas ça, qu'ils aillent ailleurs! Nous sommes des pauvres, au service des pauvres. Espérons qu'ils trouveront ici leur maison. (30)

When it comes time for Paul Delance to speak, he upsets his listeners by telling them that while he accepts the new multipurpose room as a good idea, he is not ready to close down the church. The architects, curates, journalists, and Communist mayor are stunned, but it is the architect, Le Récamier, who tells him that he is going to report him to the bishop. Ironically, we here find that it is a liberal who, in an inquisitional manner, is threatening to denounce the conservative. Paul, looking at an object on the wall that someone with imagination could interpret to be a crucifix, responds: "Il existe pour nous tous un super patron qui sait bien ce qu'Il veut. Et c'est Lui" (31). Once again, the battle lines are being drawn early in the novel between partisans of the old church and those of the new church.

As in *Les Nouveaux Prêtres*, the principal characters reflect differing points of view regarding the identity and mission of the Catholic Church and its relationship to society at large. There are three major points of view in this *roman d'idées*. The first is expressed by the largest group of characters, those who applaud Vatican II and are striving to implement its directives. The curates Cornelli and Leblanc are representative of the great majority of priests in the local area as well as of their bishop, Mgr Barré. The second point of view is incarnated by those characters who accept what happened at Vatican II as a historical fact that cannot be denied. At the same time, those who think like this, especially Paul Delance and Cardinal Mérignac, do not want the church to forget its pre-conciliar past or to water down its doctrine in order to make itself more acceptable to secular elements in society. The third point of view, rejection of Vatican II and the changes that it has brought, is represented by only one character, Georges Gallart, now a retired university professor. Thus, the novel, like the world that it seeks to mirror, recognizes that the vast majority of priests and laity support the changes that have taken place. Decidedly fewer people can be called "moderate" and only a clear, fringe minority can be classified as "intégriste."

It is ironic that this novel of ideas has more of a story line and moves more rapidly than several of Saint Pierre's other novels. The story, in fact, is quite simple. Paul Delance attempts to use his power as pastor of Saint Marc's to block demolition of the church and the transfer of all parish functions to the "centre œcuménique." To this end, he visits his old friend, Cardinal Mérignac. He does so in order to defend himself against Leblanc and Cornelli who have reported him to Mgr Barré. Grand ideas, high ideals, petty politics. While all the maneuvering is taking place, Paul begins to understand that he is gradually becoming a stigmatic. If, at the end of *Les Nouveaux Prêtres*, the long hours that he had spent in the confessional (where he was often able to read people's minds before they could speak to him), were reminiscent of an important part of the priestly experience of the famous curé of Ars, these new experiences are clearly modeled on those of another of Saint Pierre's heroes, Padre Pio (1887-1968), the Italian priest who lived with the stigmata for fifty-seven years, but who was never officially recognized by Rome.[9]

In the meantime, Barré and his cohorts organize a "commission d'enquête" to investigate Delance in order to discredit him and have him dismissed from his functions. But by the time the report is finished and ready to be sent to the Cardinal, Barré will have fallen ill with cancer. Before he dies, however, he calls Paul to his bedside to ask him to hear his confession and to tell him that he has decided to drop the investigation and ask Mérignac to allow Paul to remain at Saint Marc's. But it is too late, for Barré's successor, a former activist in the Action Catholique social movement, has already been appointed. Paul Delance has been dismissed as pastor and Cornelli named to take his place. As the novel ends, Paul Delance is leaving Paris destined for the hospital in the south of France that he has founded with money donated by his many benefactors. Here, he feels, he will be out of everyone's way. He has been stripped of everything: his parish, his confessional, the two children, Camille and François, whom he had miraculously cured, and the friendship of Barré in the latter's final days. Reminiscent of the closing words, "Tout est grâce," uttered by the curé d'Ambricourt in Bernanos's *Journal d'un curé de campagne*, the novel concludes: "Paul continuait de se taire. Il sentait revenir la cruelle douleur de sa tête, et les marques sanglantes, à son front, commençaient d'apparaître. C'était la grâce, avec la couronne d'épines" (247).

Pierre de Boisdeffre admitted at the outset of his review of the novel in the *Revue des Deux Mondes* that despite his admiration for Saint Pierre's work, especially *Les Aristocrates* and *Ce Monde ancien*, "le combat politique et religieux qui est le sien depuis vingt ans a rendu pour moi difficile une critique équitable de ses livres."[10] Boisdeffre goes on to say that he admires the novel, but with reservations, the major one being the introduction, directly and without nuance, of the subject of miracles.

In modern times, the Catholic Church has tended to lend a deaf ear to claims of miraculous occurrences. From the apparitions at Fatima and Lourdes to Padre Pio (on whose behalf a devoted group of followers and disciples, is seeking official beatification by the church), ecclesiastical reaction has usually been characterized by initial skepticism, followed by a refusal to make any official statement about claims made. In modeling Paul Delance after Padre Pio and placing him in the social context of a Paris suburb (whereas Padre Pio spent virtually his entire adult life in a monastery), Saint Pierre is taking a calculated risk. It is well known that one of the things that he holds against Vatican II is his belief that the post-conciliar church is reluctant to talk about spiritual, let alone, miraculous events and realities. Thus, in reaction to the modern church liberals and "progressistes" who so often declare in real life, as well as in Saint Pierre's novels "plus de surnaturel," he is trying to confront his reader with a direct presentation of spiritual realities at the very heart of his novel. In so doing, he is writing what we consider to be a Catholic novel in the full sense of the term. Not only does it raise spiritual questions that are typically Catholic, it also does so in a social and political real life context that is decidedly Catholic. In all fairness, however, we ought to recall that Saint Pierre conveniently overlooks the historical fact that the church's refusal to take seriously miraculous claims has existed throughout the recent modern era preceding the Council, and did not originate in the sixties.

The "commission d'enquête" mentioned above is in fact as much concerned with Paul's psychological balance as with anything else. His refusal to go along with the dedication of the new ecumenical center and his blind attachment to the preservation of the parish church are one aspect of the problem. Furthermore, he has cured a local blind girl and in the process lost his own sight. Another cure is claimed by a local mother whose paralyzed four year old son, François, began to walk again after he had been touched by a garment blessed by Paul. She has made much of this alleged cure and the press, including TV and radio, have picked up the story, going so far as to try to interview Paul—without success. Of course, he also continues to say the outlawed Latin mass, which in itself is an act of insubordination to his bishop. When these facts are added to the evidence of the stigmata, the "commission d'enquête," consisting principally of three doctors, concludes that this is a classic case of a psychosomatic disorder and that he is "un cas de névrose avancée" (280). Paul Delance is thus an official embarrassment even to those who believe in the supernatural origins of his experience. He will have to leave the Paris area.

It is precisely this forthright introduction of the miraculous that caused a shrewd and experienced reader like Pierre de Boisdeffre to have reservations about the novel: "Avouons-le très simplement," he writes, "ce recours au miracle nous gêne."[11] For him, the novel is weakened by the fact that the conflict between the old church and the new church is too polarized—and we might add that it is considerably more polarized than in *Les Nouveaux Prêtres*. In trying to show these tensions, Saint Pierre implies that anyone with reservations about certain initiatives and excesses of the new church should feel at home in the old church as represented by Paul Delance. But the situation is much more nuanced than this and in the final analysis the post-conciliar church of 1978, with all the stimulating and exciting things happening in it, does not appear in this novel. It is as if the novelist had been blinded—or did not want to see—all the post-conciliar energy and vigor around him. As Pierre de Boisdeffre puts it:

Je ne reconnais pas L'Eglise catholique aujourd'hui, dans sa diversité, dans sa richesse foisonnante, dans ses divisions mêmes, à travers cette simplification, presque caricaturale. Je ne consens pas à la réduire à cet affrontement mythique d'un homme de Dieu frappé des stigmates de la Passion et de clercs déboussolés.[12]

Whereas the contrast in *Les Nouveaux Prêtres* had remained more evenhanded, despite the fact that few critics at the time were able to appreciate this fact, *La Passion* gives a somewhat different impression. Written at a time when the new church had triumphed over and replaced the old church in the minds of the overwhelming majority of the Catholic population in France, the novel creates a tension that is difficult to respond to positively. In a generally secular and skeptical age, the example of Padre Pio means little to the average reader and a priest of this kind bears little or no resemblance to priests with whom the average reader can identify. The Paul Delance of *Les Nouveaux Prêtres*, however, whose extraordinary powers are limited to his ability to see into people's hearts and souls, is much more credible. Finally, when Pierre de Boisdeffre writes: "Bref, sur un sujet aussi grave, j'aurais souhaité plus de nuances; dès qu'il s'agit de psychologie, tout est dans la nuance,"[13] we cannot help but agree with him. Although *La Passion* remains a very interesting and engaging book to read, it is this lack of nuance that ultimately causes it to fail as a Catholic novel.

At the same time, it was another attempt by Saint Pierre to write a novel that was specifically Catholic in that it revolved around issues rooted in Catholic theology and devotional practice. It is no doubt significant that Bernanos is quoted a number of times by characters in the novel and that the last line of the work, containing the phrase "c'était la grâce," deliberately attempts to evoke in the reader's mind the *dénouement* of Bernanos's *Journal d'un curé de campagne*. But whereas the latter novel gives much more weight to spiritual and mystical questions, and is concerned only secondarily with social and political ones, Saint Pierre's *Passion* tries to give equal attention to all these questions. There can be no doubt that he is quite successful, as he had been in *Les Nouveaux Prêtres*, in analyzing the social and political stands of the three main types of Catholics mentioned, but he succeeds less well in presenting the spiritual and mystical realities that interest him. Despite these reservations, we cite once again Pierre de Boisdeffre's assessment of the work, expressed in another review of the novel, as one with which we agree: "On peut—c'est mon cas—ne point partager le combat, politique et religieux, de Michel de Saint Pierre. On ne peut pas être insensible à la force, à la conviction entraînante de ce beau roman, qui sera violemment attaqué mais qui marquera une date."[14]

Finally, Robert Poulet sums up Saint Pierre's dilemma when he writes that although it is possible to create the feeling of spiritual reality in a reader's mind, it is much more difficult, if not impossible, to create the impression of the specifically miraculous. Concluding his review of the novel, he states:

> J'ai beaucoup parlé du sujet que traite Michel de Saint Pierre et peu de son livre, parce que tout cela est très important—même pour les non croyants. Je me hâte pourtant d'ajouter que ce livre est noble et beau, bien accablé sous le poids d'une tâche impossible, littérairement parlant. Seul le miracle peut rendre compte du miracle, dans le cœur de chaque homme pris à part. Que le lecteur tente sa chance quand même, qu'il tende l'oreille. Il faudrait qu'il perçût lui-même le grondement du chien monstrueux qui hantait les nuits du curé d'Ars.[15]

8. Late Reflections on a Society in Crisis

THE PRINCIPAL INSPIRATION FOR *LAURENT*[1] WAS THE SUICIDE OF SAINT Pierre's son, Richard, in 1979. In view of this fact, the novel takes on added meaning, since throughout its pages we see the author striving to understand the younger generation that is passing through university age a decade or so after the "events" of 1968. As one might suspect, the novel also touches on some of the issues raised twenty years earlier in *Les Nouveaux Aristocrates,* but the transformation of French society (that is, the modernization in the American sense of more creature comforts, more leisure time, and less of a sense of family and tradition), during this time period makes detailed comparisons difficult if not impossible. The adolescents in their last year of secondary school in *Les Nouveaux Aristocrates* still went to school in an atmosphere in which the classical notions of order and beauty prevailed. Now, in Laurent, the twenty-two-year-olds who are enrolled at the Paris Faculté de Droit live in a world in which these classical concepts mean little or nothing. Instead, going to class in blue jeans and imitation American-style sweat shirts, listening exclusively to rock and disco music, and allowing themselves to become obsessed with the achievement of material rewards, they laugh at the idea of duty to society or service to their fellow man. The new society with its ideal of full employment and ever-increasing consumption is the only one that they have ever known.

In Saint Pierre's view, the principal losses sustained here are reflected in the lack of goals that characterizes these young adults. Since the state asks nothing of them (except to eventually become consumers), they do not know what duty or patriotism are. Since the family in France has been in a state of decline, with more and more divorces and fewer and fewer parents able to communicate effectively with their children, the young people wander in and out of emotional relationships and experiment with drugs in a manner that one would not be surprised to find, say, in California, but hardly in tradition-bound France.

A few years prior to the publication of *Laurent*, Saint Pierre had offered his opinion on this post-1968 generation of French youth. By the time the novel was written, at the end of the seventies, this thinking was still operative:

> Dans *l'Ecole de la violence*, j'avais annoncé les événements de 68 avec six ans d'avance . . . Les jeunes, ce sont des Martiens: leur structure mentale n'est pas la nôtre. Autrefois, elle s'appuyait en s'opposant: une certaine tradition restait respectée. Aujourd'hui, les jeunes, y compris mes propres enfants, mes Martiens, refusent la société en bloc: ils s'opposent à tout, du progrès à la pollution.[2]

Laurent is one of these "Martians," and his story is not a happy one.

The novel is structured around the relationships of two couples, Laurent de Balivière and Sylvaine Pizzario, and Pierre-Yves Derisle and Charlotte Lindermann. As the action begins, Pierre-Yves, who is studying photography, and Charlotte, a law student, have decided to live together. At this time we also find Sylvaine, who possesses a brilliant intellect and for whom success at the law faculty comes quite easily, attempting to convince Laurent to accept her love. Unfortunately, she will be unsuccessful in her efforts, because Laurent, also a gifted student, is alienated from everyone, including his brother, his sister, and his parents, and cannot be reached in a personal, let alone, intimate, way.

Modeled on Richard de Saint Pierre, Laurent is the scion of an aristocratic family. His mother, loving and generous and always willing to listen when he feels that he has something to tell her, is referred to by him as "la Reine-Mère." His father, a renowned poet and man of letters who, thanks to his personal fortune and income from writing, can afford a large, eight-room apartment in a fashionable section of Paris, wants to establish contact with his oldest son but is frustrated by the fact that communication always seems to break down between them.

Raised in the traditional manner, that is, in the belief that social and economic privilege must always be linked to the idea of service to others, Charles-Alfred de Balivière often refers to these young people, Laurent and his friends, as "Martiens." They are citizens of a different universe and speak a different language. To the elder Balivière, too many of their values, especially their materialism, have been imported from the United States and have been haphazardly grafted onto them. Thus, they prefer to drink Coca-Cola, not wine; they practice free love without any hint of the sexual jansenism that reigned in their social milieu in earlier generations; and, finally, they dress in jeans and wear "California University" sweatshirts to school instead of the traditional jacket and tie. The new France of President, Giscard d'Estaing, the so-called "République libérale avancée," will need leaders who are first and foremost technocrats capable of leading their country in peaceful economic competition against the U.S., Germany, and Japan. This new elite may well prove to be able to do this at some point in the future, but for the time being it is apparent that they have not received, either from their parents or their schools, a sense of rootedness and an appreciation for their French traditions. "La croissance exige l'enracinement. L'éducation devrait tendre à cela d'abord. J'aime le mot 'racine:' il me parle de terre, d'équilibre et de vie" (164), states the elder Balivière in an article that he is preparing for publication. To him, all sense of rootedness has been taken away from these young people by the rapid grafting of the computer age onto a society that had been the least advanced of the world's great powers twenty-five years earlier. This loss of roots has been shattering for French youth. Because of the power of this theme and the way it is presented in the novel, *Laurent* resembles certain of the earlier novels, especially *Les Nouveaux Aristocrates*, in that the reader does not get the clear sense of a beginning, a middle, and an end, but rather of an atmosphere, a general situation, an overwhelming malaise, that is described from varying points of view. The situation here can be called "modern French youth," or to use a much abused term, "the problem of the generation gap."

This latter theme had already been explored in *Ce Monde ancien*, *La Mer à boire,* and *Les Ecrivains*, but here Saint Pierre takes the analysis several steps further. Sharing with his reader through the character of Charles-Alfred de Balivière the frustration of a parent who cannot communicate with his son, he achieves a touching level of pathos in this novel. Language is a prime ingredient in this estrangement between father and son, and it functions in at least two significant ways. First, the vulgarity of everyday speech and the willing use of slang by these privileged young people are disconcerting. Despite all their advantages, they still speak to each other in a vulgar idiom. As the elite of the rising generation, the hope of the nation's future, they signal their alienation from their parents' values by their usual way of speaking among themselves. Secondly, when someone like Laurent does cross over and talk to his parents, he must use their language, but even when he does, he is unable to give importance, even basic meaning, to words that mean so much to them like family, faith, duty, and tradition. As Laurent becomes more difficult to understand, it is because of this basic breakdown in communication. And as the opportunities to exchange words diminish, his temptation to end his life and find a safe haven of silence will increase.

In addition to the opinions of M. de Balivière on the students' predicament, we are also shown the reactions of two professors at the law faculty, one who is older and nearing retirement age, the other one in the early years of his career. Added to this are the reactions and opinions of the students themselves. With regard to the latter, it must be recalled, however, that they do not represent a cross-section of society. Rather, they are all from the upper bourgeoisie, the children of high ranking civil servants and professional men. Thus, they belong to the traditional elite of French society, which, despite the many changes made in the educational system since 1968, still maintains its position of leadership and its privileges. As we get to know these young people and listen in on their conversations, we learn that their primary concern is security: to get the university degree that will open the door to a secure job. This consideration seems to be at least as important as the amount of money they will earn. They generally feel alienated by their studies, which they justifiably consider to be dry and boring in large part because the teaching methods employed are backward looking and poorly adapted to the new society in which they live.

This feeling of estrangement and of poor communication is reflected as well in the feelings of Professor Grenu-Chazal, who has devoted his whole life to teaching law. Enjoying complete job security and commanding a handsome salary, he confides to his wife that he no longer enjoys teaching because all that his students want out of life is a secure job. He wants to open their minds to the exploration of philosophical questions within the context of the law, but the students pay no attention to him.

The other, younger, faculty member is Stanislas Martin. He is idealistic and, like many faculty members of his generation, available to his students outside of class. They generally appreciate this willingness to get to know them as individuals, but this can sometimes lead to problems, as in the case of Sylvaine, who seeks to enter his circle of friends in the hope that she will be invited to share his bed. Martin's familiarity and openness are complicated by the fact that he wears his magistrate's robes to class and repeatedly tells them that despite the fact that they find themselves living in a new type of society, they must all establish in their lives a personal goal that is larger than themselves and employ their individual freedom to attain it. Invoking the traditional classical values of order and beauty, he tells them that they should be guided by a "double exigence esthétique et morale—et que cette exigence reste à hauteur d'étoile" (263). To do otherwise is to risk failure, because "une génération obsédée par la securité de l'emploi ne ferait pas avancer d'un pas l'humanité" (262).

Laurent is presented to us against this background of changing value systems, and the reader cannot help but sympathize with him as he attempts to decide whether to end his life or to continue to go through the motions in a world devoid of meaning. Central to the lack of communication between Laurent and his father is their disagreement about religion. Charles-Alfred considers himself to be essentially a pagan and that mankind in general is basically corrupt and selfish. But because of his Catholic faith, he is able to transcend these limitations and give a meaning to his life. Like Pascal, he is wagering that life has a hidden meaning to it and that its meaning coincides with the tenets of traditional Catholicism. Laurent, on the other hand, is willing to concede that there might very well be a God somewhere, but he rejects the idea of an institutional church and thus no longer feels an obligation to attend mass or receive the sacraments. He tells his father that he admires St. Augustine and finds the Gospel of St. John to be beautiful poetry, but that is as far as he can go. Studying Roman law and reading Montherlant, who was fascinated by suicide for many years before finally deciding to take his own life, Laurent has come to admire and believe in what he calls "l'homme antique" who was able to invent and impose on the world the Pax Romana. What attracts him in pagan man is "sa hiérarchie des valeurs, son socialisme en action et son courage de ne croire en rien." (155) Although he admits to a certain admiration for Catholicism, he voices his disillusion with what he calls "la navrante civilisation chrétienne." This comment provokes a rejoinder from his father about what has happened to French society since the Revolution:

> Désolé, Laurent; il n'y a plus de civilisation chrétienne. Le libéralisme
> à la mode de nos trois dernières républiques, et le socialisme—
> n'importe quel socialisme—sont fondamentalement anti-chrétiens. Tu

ne vas pas comparer ces amuse-gueules à ce que fût l'Occident catholique, j'espère! Et je m'en vais te dire une bonne chose: toute
civilisation dont le Christ n'est pas le maître aboutit fatalement par sa
force brutale ou par sa faiblesse, au Goulag. Autrement dit: à la mort.
(156)

In view of this basic disagreement, Charles-Alfred once again
attempts to establish contact with his son by writing him a long letter in
which he states his beliefs. To him, the Beatitudes as stated in St. Matthew's Gospel are the centerpiece of Catholicism. He writes:

Ecoute-moi bien, comme chaque homme sur la terre, j'ai connu dans
ma vie des peines très dures. Mais quand la coupe de la souffrance est
trop pleine, je pense à ce langage étrange et fou des Béatitudes, que nul
homme avant le Christ n'avait jamais tenu; j'y baigne la violence de
ma nature, et je m'apaise de savoir que beaucoup plus durement que
moi, le Dieu des Béatitudes est devenu l'homme de la Croix. Heureux
ceux qui souffrent persécution pour la justice! (160)

Unfortunately, the letter will not have the desired effect and father and son,
although respectful of each other, will remain estranged through the end of
the novel.

After receiving the letter, Laurent takes it along with him to Charlotte's apartment and reads it to her. Charlotte dismisses the letter as the
work of a religious fanatic. But her reaction only causes him to defend his
father as a person, even though he cannot share what his father calls "la foi
des anciens jours" (177). Having sought a new faith by becoming a member of the Socialist Party, that experience, like everything else, has also led
to disappointment.

Another last attempt at communication comes when Laurent takes
his mother aside, telling her that he has to talk to her. He feels depressed
and finds no reason to go on living. Again and again, he talks of death and
of silence. He has lost interest in his work at school, where he excels with
little effort, as well as in writing poetry, where he shows great promise.
When she tells him to keep on reading St. John's Gospel in the hope that it
will help him to find some meaning in life, he dismisses her request. "Saint
Jean, c'est de la poésie pure" (216), he tells her, implying that it can have
no practical value for him and his feelings of estrangement. When this final

attempt at communication fails, suicide as a solution to his problem becomes an even more tangible alternative.

Unable to find any reason to go on living, Laurent finally decides to end his life. He places a revolver in his mouth. There is only one shell in its six chambers. He pulls the trigger twice but nothing happens. Impatient, and feeling claustrophobic in his room, he goes out for a walk along the river bank. He throws his eye glasses in the Seine and then, in search of a world in which there will be "ni doute ni mensonge" (274), he seems to jump in. As he does so, he thinks of his family and the note that he has left for them: "Là où je vais, je serai encore plus près de vous" (275).

But does he really jump in after all? The last two pages are written in such a way that the same Laurent who is about to jump in the river is depicted a few sentences later returning home, soaked with water. Is this a dream that we are seeing, either Laurent's, or perhaps that of his parents, or is he really alive and well? The ending is equivocal and some critics have concluded that Saint Pierre, as a Catholic novelist, could not bring himself to allow a character to commit suicide. They are correct. Saint Pierre has held out for a happy—or at least hopeful—outcome to the novel. This vision of Laurent running home to his mother reminds us of the theme of maternal love that is so strong in so many of the earlier novels, like *Ce Monde ancien*, *La Mer à boire*, and *Les Nouveaux Prêtres*, as well as of how devastating it can be when young people are deprived of their mothers, like the Marquis de Maubrun's children or young Georges Damville. Happily, Laurent does not die here, but the fact that he has been driven to take such extreme action is serious enough. The attempt, in other words, is more important than whether or not he succeeds.

Laurent once again confirms Saint Pierre's interest in young adults as a subject of a novel. From *Ce Monde ancien* and *La Mer à boire*, through *Les Nouveaux Aristocrates*, to *Laurent*, he returns to their problems in adapting themselves to a society that has changed more since 1945 than during any other forty-year period in French history. The traditional French notion of the generation gap as expressed in the saying "on s'appuie en s'opposant," no longer applies here because these youngsters are truly "Martians" in the eyes of their parents. They speak a language that is different from the one used by their elders and they have a different value system. Interestingly, in earlier novels with a generic title—*Les Ecrivains* is an excellent example—Saint Pierre used an all-inclusive title but really only focused on one individual writer and not on writers as a group. Here he seems to be trying to do just the opposite, for despite the title of the novel and the centrality of Laurent's experiences to the workings of the book, the novel also seeks to depict the state of mind and the way of life of a whole generation of young men and women from France's social elite.

Of all of Saint Pierre's novels, this one represents perhaps best of all what we have referred to as the cinematic quality of his style. He tells a story rapidly, in scenes that are vividly set, but without employing lengthy descriptions. The dialogue is hard hitting, and the Latin Quarter slang reverberates in the reader's mind. Psychological analysis, instead of being presented in authorial overvoicing, is portrayed most often in language and gesture: for example, Laurent's loss of equilibrium being portrayed through his use of vulgar slang as he talks to his mother while licking up with his tongue the jam that has fallen from his muffin to his plate. Significantly, it was this very quality that struck Pierre de Boisdeffre in the novel: "Quel beau dialogue de théâtre on pourrait tirer de ce récit . . ."[3] he wrote.

In the final analysis, Laurent is as personal a novel as any that Michel de Saint Pierre has written. Like the two early novels that were based essentially on his own personal experience and less on Balzacian-style documentation, this one gives us as much of the writer himself as one can expect. In trying to give voice to the tragic elements in Laurent's pathetic adventure, it touches us in a way that none of his other books do.

Docteur Erikson[4] contains an interesting three-page introduction by Saint Pierre in which he thanks those doctors who have helped him either personally or through their books. He tells us that he has immersed himself in the controversy surrounding new methods of treating cancer and that he wants to acknowledge his debts publicly. He also adds that he has embarked upon "un vaste programme" in devoting himself as a novelist to becoming an "écrivain témoin de son temps." Having been tempted for a time as a young man to study medicine, he finally decided instead on a career as a writer. Now having reached the age of sixty-five, he reminds us of the subjects that he has treated in his novels: "C'est ainsi que j'ai décrit successivement, dans mes romans, les milieux de l'usine, de la Sorbonne, des aristocrates, des écrivains et des salons littéraires, des prêtres progressistes, des affaires, des tribunaux" (13). Nearing the end of his career and looking back on it, he evidently wanted to be remembered as a witness to his age.

Significantly, he makes no mention in this preface of his vocation as an "écrivain catholique." In our view, this should not be surprising, since the two goals are not mutually exclusive. As mentioned above, if we take Bernanos and Mauriac as examples, it is evident that the genuine Catholic writer cannot help also being a commentator on the age in which he lives. The moral insights that prop up his fictions are also valid in the real world. But we must also bear in mind that for a writer like Saint Pierre, who made his living and supported his family on income from his books, the epithet "écrivain témoin de son temps" was attractive because it was more inclusive and less parochial than that of "écrivain catholique." In addition, Saint Pierre's forthright and outspoken positions on public issues had categorized him over several decades in the mind of the French public as a traditionalist Catholic. From his positions on keeping Algeria French in the sixties, through the seventies when he spoke out against what he took to be Marxist influences among the French clergy, to the early eighties when he was on the barricades fighting against the Socialist proposal to nationalize France's Catholic schools, Saint Pierre's name was continually associated with traditional, right-wing Catholicism. Thus, in striving to underline his calling as a novelist who is a witness to his age, he was not denying the Catholic element in his inspiration, which was essential to his work and his life, but only attempting to clarify the fact that as a novelist he was committed to describing the world as he saw it.

We might also add that his major concerns and interests since *Les Nouveaux Prêtres* had become so broad in scope that this newer epithet, "witness to his age," seems to fit quite well. In addition, the definition of the word "catholique" as an adjective used to define the French church, has changed quite drastically since Vatican II. The new church has opened itself to the world, and Catholics, who by definition are the church, reflect this opening, which has also involved a political shift to the left by both clergy and faithful. This fact highlights one of the ironies in Saint Pierre's fictional œuvre as we read his last novels. For although Saint Pierre the pamphleteer and public person remained a highly visible spokesman for traditional pre-Vatican II Catholicism, his novels generally embraced the new, post-Vatican II world view. In this fictional universe, he surely does not praise or approve of all the changes that have taken place in French society and the French church over the past twenty years, but at the same time, he represents and analyzes them fairly and accurately without really expressing any desire to turn the clock back to an earlier age. Thus, the introductory pages of *Docteur Erikson* quoted above are important as an indication of how Saint Pierre, reaching the twilight of his career, saw himself and his work.

One of the first things that strikes us about the hero of *Docteur Erikson* is his personal revolt against "la médecine officielle" (22). As the novel opens, we meet a young couple in their early thirties who have moved from Paris to a fictional provincial town near Evreux in Normandy called Fleury-sur-Risle. They have been there for three months. Erikson has bought a small house outside town, and he is counting on continued industrial growth in the region to provide a clientele for his private practice. His specialty is a combination of general practice and "phytothérapie," which is defined as "soins des maladies infectueuses par les plantes et par les huiles essentielles" (19). Erikson had been tempted at one time to specialize either in pneumology or cardiology, but both disciplines are already overcrowded and, in addition, the latter has become too technical. Seeing himself as what the French like to call a "littéraire," rather than as a "scientifique" (22), that is, someone with a broad humanist bent rather than a narrow scientific one, he has finally decided on a specialty in which he can use all his gifts as a human being. This decision also dictates self-imposed exile from Paris where the "médecine officielle" reigns and where his freedom to practice this new type of medecine would be severely restricted.

Erikson has already been married for several years to Armèle, whose mother is Chinese and whose father is French. Raised in Taiwan, she speaks English and Chinese as well as French and enjoys a "petite fortune personnelle" that allows her a good deal of independence from her husband. It is she who has actually paid for their old farmhouse and is now financing its restoration and modernization. Guillaume Erikson has thus assumed the financial responsibility for setting up his medical practice, but beyond that his financial worries are limited. The relative independence of each partner is reinforced by the fact that they have no children, even though they have been attempting to become parents during their five years of married life. This situation, that is, a childless couple at the heart of a novel, is an anomalous one in Saint Pierre's fiction, because throughout his career he has repeatedly displayed his interest in portraying family life, excelling at times in painting the communication difficulties that sometimes exist between parents and children. The only other one of his novels in which family life, or at least a serious parent-child relationship, is not depicted, is *Les Nouveaux Prêtres*. This fact in itself tells us how important the doctor's vocation is to Saint Pierre: like the priest, he is specially called to struggle against evil, here named "l'Ennemi."

Erikson, however, even at the beginning of the novel, is not happily married. The principal reason for this malaise is that his wife takes absolutely no interest in his work. For a long time he had thought that he would be able to live two lives, one devoted to medecine and the other to his wife, with a "rideau d'acier" (58) firmly separating the two. Now he knows that this is impossible and he longs to share his professional concerns with his wife. But at the same time, he presumes that his work comes first and Armèle only second. Thus, he never hesitates to be late for a meal or to miss one altogether without even bothering to notify her. The most important thing that they do seem to have in common is a mutual physical attraction, but it is unclear as the novel begins whether this will be enough to sustain their marriage. After five years of a shared existence, the only thing that Erikson is sure of about his wife is her erotic nature: inevitably, the reader cannot help but think of Emma Bovary, that other Norman housewife, herself the creation of a Norman novelist.

Early in the novel, as Erikson is busy setting up his office, Armèle makes the acquaintance of a neighbor, Eric Stengalen, a young landowner and adventuresome bachelor. He invites Armèle to go horseback riding with him. Flattered by the invitation, and with plenty of spare time on her hands, she accepts. But when she invites Eric over for dinner to meet her husband, the latter suspects that something has gone wrong, that he is losing touch with his wife, and his reaction in swift. A few days later, he pays an unannounced visit to Stengalen at the latter's home to tell him to stay away from Armèle. This is the end of the potentially adulterous relationship between Armèle and her neighbor, at the same time as it serves as a warning to Armèle and Erikson that they are badly in need of improved modes of communication. Gradually, and without ever really discussing the matter, she begins to take more interest in his work while, at the same time, he seems to be more willing to ask for, and to follow, her advice.

The relationship between Erikson and his wife, although essential to the novel, is still secondary to the main concern of the book, which is the war waged against cancer, the great, unchecked illness of the developed world, by the victims that it attacks and the doctors and scientists who dare to challenge it. The cancer cell, described over and over again throughout the novel, represents "l'Ennemi." It invades the healthy human organism unannounced and for reasons that cannot be adequately explained. Its arrival is compared to that of a conquering army that lays waste to the land that it attacks, and its image is made all the more powerful by the recurring descriptions of fertile Norman soil, "la terre normande," in which the action is set. Erikson, a blue-eyed, blond descendent of the Vikings, like Marc Van Hussel of *La Mer à boire* and Bruno Martinville of *Je reviendrai*, has left Paris to plant himself in the land of his ancestors. Like the land itself, each human victim is a perfect whole that is overwhelmed by seemingly blind forces of devastation. The whole person, and not just one or several organs, is affected by this onslaught. Thus, the patient can only be cared for and cured by a treatment that calls for a complete plan of rehabilitation, not by piecemeal and sporadic attempts to cure only one or several aspects of the disorder. Examining a forty year old woman whose stomach cancer has returned after surgery and radiological treatment, Erikson thinks of an invading army and helpless defenders:

> Regardant sa visiteuse, il songeait à cette invasion d'un organisme encore jeune—d'un terrain vivant que l'on n'avait pas irrigué ni protégé: le mal pouvait évoluer pendant des années. De ce corps déjà vaincu qu'il affectait d'examiner avec soin, les cellules malignes prendraient possession inexorablement, reduisant une à une les défenses et massacrant les défenseurs . . . Guillaume ne pensait qu'à l'Ennemi, installé, fortifié au centre d'une vie qu'il s'acharnait à détruire, comme s'il poursuivait avec intelligence un grand dessein. (69-70)

Saint Pierre introduces a specifically Catholic dimension to the novel by relating the diabolical nature of "l'Ennemi,"cancer, to the metaphysical concerns of the nineteenth century French novelist Barbey d'Aurévilly.[5] Erikson has been asked to write a preface for a new edition of Barbey's works that will be brought out by a small regional publishing house devoted to re-editing the works of Norman writers. Thus, superficially, Barbey and Erikson are related because they are Normans, but this link is a symbol of a deeper, more spiritual affinity. Erikson hangs engravings of Barbey in the waiting room at his office and is fascinated by the author of *Les Diaboliques* (1874) who, like him, was attracted by the mysterious nature of evil as it works hidden beneath the alluring veneer of human life.

The second of the two major themes is the reaction of man when confronted by the presence of evil as represented by cancer. Basically, there are four different reactions delineated in the novel, each one reflecting the point of view of a practicing specialist: surgeons, chemotherapists, radiologists and biologists. As the novel progresses, it becomes clear that the author's warmest sympathy is reserved for the latter group (as well as for the doctors who are courageous enough to work with them), since their philosophical approach is holistic in nature and attempts to fortify the whole body and to nurture its innate defense capabilities.

Although Erikson sees a large number of patients with gastric, intestinal, and liver problems (due to the large amounts of cream, cider, and calvados ingested by the local inhabitants), he takes special interest in his cancer patients. Several case histories are treated in detail, but the most important one is that of Jacques Lesmanerie, a middle-aged and otherwise healthy man who suffers from a cancerous tumor of the esophagus. Erikson orders that it be removed, but then adds that there will be no follow-up radiation and chemotherapy treatments because their side effects are so powerful and because they do not address the real problem as he, Erikson, sees it. Instead, he counsels a positive mental attitude to be buttressed by a treatment in accordance with his specialty, *phytothérapie*.

After the operation at the local hospital where the surgeon, Dr. Saint-Marcellin, reigns, the resident radiologist and chemotherapist each demand sole responsibility for treating Lesmanerie. But Erikson refuses, claiming that the surgery is sufficient and that now is the time to build up the body's natural defenses. To bolster his own position, he establishes contact with a former classmate from Paris, Gilles Dupont des Riaux, an independent-minded researcher who, while still a student, earned the wrath of their eminent professor, Barley-Dumesny, by rejecting the traditional cancer treatments of surgery, radiation, and chemotherapy, in favor of a biological approach. When he learns that Dupont, working with the researcher Le Prédieux, has been using a substance called D50 to treat cancer patients, he decides to try it on Lesmanerie. Le Prédieux has fashioned the drug from extracts taken from healthy animal tissues and has had good results with the treatment for a number of years. The D50 is administered immediately to Lesmanerie, and the treatment goes well for several months. At this point, Erikson, his friend Dupont des Riaux, and the biologist Le Prédieux organize a meeting at the latter's home in order to present to several members and representatives of "la médecine officielle" important information on the tangible results obtained by several different doctors working quietly and discreetly with D50 and the related drug D80. But the meeting ends in failure, for none of the observers favoring traditional treatment can be persuaded by the evidence presented. Even worse, as the novel moves toward its conclusion, representatives of the medical establishment, working through the medical association, the Conseil de l'Ordre des Médecins, attempt to have Erikson's license revoked for treating a patient with unauthorized drugs. In the final few pages, as he is readying his defense, Erikson is visited by Dr. Saint-Marcellin, who had performed the surgery on Lesmanerie and heretofore had shown himself to be very skeptical of Erikson's new methods of treatment. But now Saint-Marcellin has been diagnosed as having cancer of the kidney, "une tumeur rénale maligne" (277), and he asks Erikson to treat him with D50. With this request, it becomes clear that Erikson has finally made the breakthrough that will save his career and at the same time allow him to continue to carry out his research.

All through the final chapters of the novel, Erikson is presented as a latter-day version of his Viking ancestors. While preparing to defend himself against his professional detractors, he is described as follows: "Il secoua ses mèches blondes, dardant vers Armèle son regard aigu et clair de Viking" (272). And once he is sure of victory, "son visage de guerrier blond, restait immobile" (281). Erikson's combative spirit against overwhelming odds, his courage in taking on the whole medical establishment because he is convinced that he is right and they are wrong, is portrayed here as a typically Viking, that is, courageous, trait.

At the same time, this Viking is not without a certain religious sensibility. Although we cannot say that Erikson is a Christian, questions of a religious nature regularly arise in his mind. We know, for instance, that Erikson is aware that he uses the world "God" in daily speech, as in terms like "Dieu merci," or "s'il plaît à Dieu" (200). But he also realizes that "Dieu n'est pour moi qu'une locution machinale. Mais quelle hérédité chargée nous avons! Une hérédité chrétienne, tenace comme un champignon!" (200). He is thus not unaware of Catholicism and its doctrinal claims, for after all, Armèle, whose Chinese mother is described as a "super-catholique" (p. 43), was presumably raised as a Catholic herself. But Erikson's problem is that of many modern men. Untouched by grace, he has not yet set aside the time to think about God; the pressure involved in establishing himself in his career is too great, and it absorbs all available energy. Like Marc in *La Mer à boire*, "Guillaume avait décidé de remettre à plus tard les problèmes des origines et ceux de la vie future" (200).

Hostile to the doctrinaire rationalism that dominates scientific circles, Erikson is by temperament open to and respectful of life's mysteries. How else can we explain his willingness to do battle with cancer or to devote so much of his time to reading Barbey? The last time that he discusses this interest in Barbey is with the writer Martial Thomas, a patient who has a home in the area. A member of the French Academy and a practicing Catholic, Thomas has read an excerpt from Erikson's preface to the re-edition of Barbey's work and finds it to be "excellente" (196). His own interests converge with Erikson's in so far as they are both interested in dealing with invisible realities. Also, like Saint Pierre himself, he is trying to find the spiritual life hidden beneath the grim facade of modernity. Thus, he tells the doctor about his latest book, entitled *L'Ame de la matière:*

> je spécule sur la vie électrique intense qui charge une pierre "inerte" comme nous disons, et qui la fait frémir sous nos yeux aveugles. Dans un autre ordre, je rêve autour des souffles de l'Esprit. Par exemple, j'essaie de rendre tangible cette accumulation des prières muettes et des chants liturgiques entre le sol et les voûtes de nos plus vieilles églises. Et ces jaillissements immobiles dont nos cathédrales sont remplies. . . . (201)

Thus, on one level, *Docteur Erikson* is a pamphlet calling for more tolerance for those who seek to use new, innovative methods in fighting the great killer of our age, cancer. Reviews of the novel, as well as the scores of newspaper articles written about it, obviously point to this fact. But at the same time, it recounts a spiritual journey. Erikson, like the Norsemen his ancestors, is embarked on an epic quest whose exact destination is not divulged, but it is most likely found somewhere within himself. In addition, Erikson can also be taken as a form of Christ figure. Early in the novel, he saves the life of a young colleague, Dr. Yves Cléricourt who, motivated by despair, had attempted to commit suicide. Cléricourt/Lazarus is further redeemed by his savior when he joins Erikson in his practice and then, as a true disciple, replaces him several days a week when he goes off to Paris to work on his research. But Cléricourt/Lazarus will become Cléricourt/Judas when he refuses to join Erikson in his confrontation with the medical establishment, even though he deeply believes in what Erikson is doing. Likewise, the seductive Armèle is a kind of Mary Magdalen who, tempted by their neighbor, Eric Stengalen, will nonetheless stay at her husband's side and remain faithful to him. Finally, one cannot help but notice the resemblance between Erikson and his associates and Christ and his disciples, for both proclaim a message of healing to people who do not want to hear it. Of course, Erikson and his associates are not put to death, but they narrowly escape being professionally assassinated. It is for this reason, because of the growing awareness of his spiritual mission that, at the end of the novel when Armèle proposes that they go for a walk together, he insists on being alone for a moment—and she understands: "Aspirant l'air nocturne, parfaitement libre, il s'enfonça plus avant dans cette solitude qui lui donnait ses forces" (282). Like Christ going off to the mountaintop to pray alone, Guillaume Erikson must also be with himself to ponder the meaning of life.

    Docteur Erikson was a resounding triumph, both critical and popular. While in terms of sales it might very well have been as successful as *Les Nouveaux Prêtres,* it also gained widespread critical approval. Yves-Alain Favre, noting that Saint Pierre was an "écrivain témoin de son temps, qui ne s'enfuit pas dans l'imaginaire et l'intemporel, mais traite des questions importantes qui se posent aujourd'hui," expressed admiration for the novel. Impressed by how well the story is told and how real and convincing the characters are, he marvelled at Saint Pierre's ability to deal with such a serious subject in such a readable fashion. He wrote:

> Michel de Saint Pierre n'a pas écrit ce livre à la légère comme beaucoup
> d'autres romanciers ont l'habitude de faire; patiemment et soigneuse-
> ment, il s'est informé auprès de divers médecins; il a suivi un stage
> dans un laboratoire; il a fréquenté les hôpitaux; bref, lorsqu'il parle de ce
> milieu, il n'avance rien qu'il n'ait contrôlé par l'expérience et son
> témoignage acquiert alors de la gravité.

In conclusion, Favre notes that "la gravité du sujet n'offusque pas le charme romanesque," an accolade that could be applied not only to *Docteur Erikson* but to several other of Saint Pierre's more successful novels as well.[6] To Pierre de Boisdeffre, Docteur Erikson is a "roman allègre, presque gai." He arrives at this conclusion because of what can be called the book's cinematic style, which veils the serious, even terrifying, subject matter. To Boisdeffre, the novel reflects "les qualités d'écrivain qui ont valu à Michel de Saint Pierre un immense public: clarté de l'exposition, vérité des dialogues et des situations dont le côté poignant est tempéré par l'humour de l'observateur."[7]

Jacques de Ricaumont also noted that the success of the book depends to a large extent on Saint Pierre's lucid style. "Michel de Saint Pierre est un remarquable conteur," he wrote, "qui sait captiver son lecteur avec l'exposé, qui pourrait être ardu et sous sa plume demeure étonnamment vivant."[8] Likewise, Robert Poulet hailed Saint Pierre's novelistic style:

> Le talent, un talent simple, franc, droit, dont on mesure ici les effets plus que les grâces littéraires, a seul le pouvoir d'imposer au grand public . . . ce frissonnement du sentiment et de la pensée. M. de Saint Pierre doit être félicité pour cette belle réussite.

He concluded by noting that despite the "immortelles frivolités de l'esthétique," Saint Pierre is not only a superb stylist but also a writer with a warm human message to communicate to his readers: "M. de Saint Pierre veut etre *aussi* un écrivain utile, ce qui suppose une volonté d'optimisme, qui se communique à ses héros."[9]

In conclusion, *Docteur Erikson* is the masterpiece of Saint Pierre's twilight years. Almost thirty years after the publication of *Les Aristocrates*, he proved that his stylistic powers had not diminished and that he still had something of value to say to a vast audience. Presenting character through lively dialogue and psychological analysis with a minimum of detail, he continued to exploit this cinematic quality of his prose to great effect.

Saint Pierre's next novel was *Le Double Crime de l'impasse Salomon*.[10] Its opening scene clearly reveals the author's debt to Balzac and his method. Just as at the beginning of *Le Père Goriot,* for instance, where Balzac paints a detailed picture of the lodgers and their physical surroundings in "la pension Vaucquer," Saint Pierre here offers us a minute description of the neighborhood in the sixth arrondissement where the crime is about to take place. This description also serves as a structuring device, since one of the main concerns of the novel will also be to depict for the reader one aspect of the invisible life of Paris: the world of organized crime. Thus, the impassionate description of life at 9 a.m. on a beautiful April morning in the area bordering the intersection of the rue Dupin and the rue du Cherche-Midi is intended to give the reader a feeling for everyday life in the local neighborhood. We think that what we are seeing is real, and it is, but there is another invisible reality which, like a volcano, will now send shock waves to the surface. Saint Pierre, who at one time maintained an apartment on the very street described here, is obviously very well documented, à la Balzac, on its particular characteristics. When the peaceful scene is abruptly terminated by the screams of a woman who has just come upon two dead bodies, the reader is startled. The orderly surface calm has been broken by the ripple of disorder. Saint Pierre, who has revealed so many times in his fiction that the invisible can be, and often is, more real than the visible, seems to take delight in breaking the established mood in order to initiate the reader into another world about which the average citizen really knows very little.

It becomes apparent very soon in this novel that Saint Pierre has obviously done extensive research on the activities of the Paris underworld, called "Le Milieu" or "Le Mitan." Thus, he presents Paris as a city that reveals itself to both its inhabitants and its visitors in a superficial way. The theme of the city as a more or less well-ordered mechanism in which the metro is made to function on time, the streets are cleaned, and the garbage collected, is complicated by his depiction of the forces of disorder that are forever at work. One of the most pervasive and dangerous of these forces, organized crime, comes under the purview of the police who, properly trained and equipped, must defend the city and its citizens against it.

The crime that has taken place in a luxurious townhouse located in a tiny dead end street called l'impasse Salomon, is the double murder of Arnaud Leroy-Bellègue and his wife. They have been murdered—probably some time during the preceding night—in Leroy-Bellègue's second-floor office, and their bodies have been discovered only belatedly by his secretary as she reported to work at 9 a.m. the next morning.

The authorial voice now shifts its focus from the externals of the neighborhood to the minute description of police procedures upon arriving at the scene of the crime. In the process it becomes evident that is is anything but a classic detective novel, in which the investigator is invariably portrayed with odd or quirky personality traits. Instead, Saint Pierre concentrates on the aspect of routine and of patience required in the grim and somewhat banal task of establishing leads and following up on them. He is also concerned with the police hierarchy and its organization as well as with the necessarily complimentary nature of the work done by those police assigned to the local *commissariat* and those with more specialized functions, like detectives, who work out of a central office.

To offer his reader a concrete example of underworld activity in one of their specialized areas, as well as to demonstrate the police's attempt to counteract these activities, Saint Pierre has chosen to build the novel around the theft and subsequent sale of art treasures. We gradually learn that M. and Mme Leroy-Bellègue have been slain by professionals who had become aware that Leroy-Bellègue, a well-known newspaperman specializing in investigative reporting, had learned a great deal, too much in fact, about their activities. The killer, Albert Ducci, had already visited Leroy-Bellègue once at his office to warn him. Police interrogation of the neighborhood *clochard,* called Papa Litron, offers evidence about this visit and establishes Ducci as a prime suspect.

Of prime interest is the discovery of the notebook in which Leroy-Bellègue had kept notes relating to his investigation. Before we learn that it has been found in one of his jacket pockets by his son Aubin—and kept secret by him while he conducts his own personal investigation—we are led to understand the truly international dimension of this racket and how the theft of artworks from private collections is linked to seemingly reputable dealers who then resell the stolen works to other private collectors.

The principal reason why Aubin Leroy-Bellègue, a twenty-five year old law student, and his two sisters, Séverine and Alix, have not informed the police that they have found their father's notebook, is because they believe that France's judicial system has become so partial to the rights of criminals that even if the police locate, arrest, and prosecute the murderer, the culprit will be let off with a light sentence and most likely have that sentence reduced later on. This critique of the judicial system soon reveals itself to be another one of the novel's major concerns. Its articulation also reveals the author's larger concerns as an observer of life in France under the Fifth Republic. To him the hard-working, law-abiding citizen lives in a world of danger and injustice because the criminal justice system has largely broken down. Since politicians and judges show more concern about the rights of convicted criminals than they do for the victims of crime, the average person is tempted to take the law into his own hands. Thus, Séverine speaks for her brother and sister, as well as for millions of contemporary Frenchmen when she says to the police investigators, Guy Trovern and Jean Crépin:

> On lit les journaux, vous savez. Nous écoutons même les informations
> de temps en temps, le soir, quand nous n'avons rien de mieux à faire.

Et bien, si vous trouvez qu'à présent on "châtie les coupables", nous ne sommes plus d'accord. Ce que nous refusons, justement, c'est que les assassins des parents s'en tirent avec quelques années dans une prison modèle, et des permissions de sortie en primes. Mais Aubin vous a déjà dit ça. (72-73)

Essential to this viewpoint, as well as to the novel itself, is the fact that the police themselves share this opinion. Saint Pierre is careful to give us a detailed view of the police hierarchy from the *commissaire et chef de la brigade criminelle*, Gilbert Merlin, through several layers of authority, to one of his inspectors, Guy Trovern. The latter, working closely in the investigation with a policeman from the local station, Jean Crépin, will be, along with his ultimate superior, Merlin, the main protagonist of the novel. Trovern is twenty-eight years old, has a university degree and has passed the *concours,* or competitive examination, that has allowed him to become a member of the *police judiciaire*. A Breton sprung from an anticlerical family of farmers, Trovern is an atheist who believes principally in two things in life: himself and order. In fact, it is this latter yearning, to put things right wherever he sees disorder, that has inspired him to enter police work. As he tells his mistress, Catherine, "Au fond, ce qui me plaît, c'est de coincer les salopards, parce que j'aime l'ordre" (46). He has a great respect for Merlin, and this has helped him to set a practical goal in life: "devenir un grand flic, à l'instar de son super-patron Gilbert Merlin" (46). As the Leroy-Bellègue investigation takes up more and more of this time, he finds himself progressively less inclined to spend time with Catherine, a Parisian divorcee who manages a dry cleaning establishment on the outskirts of Paris. In addition, after he commences an affair with the victims' daughter, Alix, even less time will be available for the persevering Catherine. In counterpoint to Guy Trovern is Gilbert Merlin, who is presented as everything that a high-ranking police officer should be: "élégance vestimentaire. . . concision dans l'exposé des faits . . . fermeté sobre dans le ton . . . mépris total de la politique et des politiciens" (47). Merlin has noticed in Trovern a high degree of ability and dedication and has, to a certain extent, taken him under his wing. Trovern, at this point, is not quite sure, nor is the reader, but he suspects that Merlin is a practicing Catholic and that his religious beliefs have a great deal to do with the high ethical level on which he practices his *métier*. During a Sunday dinner at Merlin's home, the two men discuss their common vocation, and Trovern reveals to his boss that his desire to fight against disorder is probably his principal reason for being in law enforcement. Merlin points out to him that he is fortunate in this regard because a recent survey published in the press had indicated that most people ultimately stumble into their professions. Speaking for himself, he tells Trovern that it is not so much a desire for order as the pleasure of the hunt that satisfies him in his work.

> Tout me plaît dans le métier. La fièvre du chasseur, d'abord, qui est une fin en soi. Et puis, bien d'autres choses: l'enjeu du débat, le labyrinthe des enquêtes dont on ne sait jamais où elles vont nous mener, ce sentiment d'impuissance et d'obscurité qui nous saisit au début de chaque affaire, la lumière qui vient ensuite comme par magie, le travail d'équipe, et surtout, la décision solitaire. Ajoutons-y, si tu veux, ce voisinage perpétuel de la violence. (197-98)

The "décision solitaire" mentioned here by Merlin will turn out to be one of the keys to the novel and at the book's *dénouement* will trigger a rupture between the two men. But to understand what Merlin really means by this term, it must be clearly understood that he entertains lofty personal and professional ideals as a policeman:

> Je te disais tout à l'heure que notre métier comporte un aspect moral. Ça peut avoir l'air d'une vérité première. Mais la morale dont je parle va bien plus loin que notre éthique policière—qui, elle, reste un peu courte. Il ne s'agit pas simplement d'obéir et de commander avec honnêteté. Il s'agit, Guy, de placer notre boulot dans sa vraie place, dans un ensemble social qui est difficile à connaître. Il s'agit surtout d'être fidèles à une certaine idée que nous nous faisons de l'homme, quoi qu'il arrive . . . ce qui pour moi revient à dire: être fidèles à une certaine idée que nous faisons de notre destin. (210-02)

But when Trovern tells him that he is an atheist who does not even share his father's anticlerical faith in the Republic, Merlin asks him what set of values he calls upon when faced with a difficult decision. "A moi-même. A rien d'autre," is the response (202).

In recounting the development of the investigation of the double crime of the novel's title, Saint Pierre has the action culminate at a meeting between Trovern, Crépin, and a third agent, all posing as dealers wanting to purchase discreetly precious artworks, and Albert Ducci and his associates who have the goods that they seek. When Crépin makes a mistake during the conversation and calls Ducci by his real name instead of by his current alias, M. Durand, a shootout occurs during which Trovern's two colleagues will be killed as well as Ducci's two associates. When Trovern realizes that Ducci, who has been shot, is probably not mortally wounded and will recover from his wounds if the other police are given time to arrive, he puts his revolver to Ducci's head and pulls the trigger. His motivation seems clear and, to him anyway, is understandable. He is acting in the heat of battle. One policeman is already dead and it is obvious that Crépin is about to die of his wounds. This act can also be construed as a cold-blooded act of murder, even an execution, because he also seems to be vaguely aware of the promise that he had made to Alix Leroy-Bellègue to execute her father's murderers. But the principal reason, as he later will tell Merlin, is that "il n'était pas question pour moi de remettre Ducci entre les mains d'une justice qui semble aimer les truands. Pour moi, il s'agissait de l'une de ces ordures pleinement responsables contre lesquelles notre société n'ose même plus se protéger" (281). But Merlin remains unconvinced. "Combien de fois vous ai-je dit à tous qu'un policier n'est pas un justicier?" he asks (281). Then, in keeping with his own personal code of ethics, he tells Trovern that he will be reassigned to another office.

As the novel ends, Trovern realizes that he has no future with Alix Leroy-Bellègue and that Catherine is still available when he wants her. More than ever, he wants to remain in police work, and even though he has been transferred out of Merlin's section, he will continue to fight against "les pollutions criminelles de la Ville . . . ces désordres qu'il haïssait plus encore qu'il n'avait haï Dieu" (287).

Putting down this novel, a reader might be tempted to ask to what extent it can be considered a Catholic novel or the work of a Catholic novelist. If the Catholic novel can be said to deal mainly with the workings of grace in the life of an individual in order to describe the soul's journey toward damnation or salvation, then *Un Double Crime* is not a Catholic novel. But this does not mean that there is no Catholic dimension to the work. Merlin, as mentioned above, is a Catholic and a professional law enforcement officer of the highest caliber. His example in both capacities is essential to the construction of the novel. The only other character who explicitly springs from a Catholic background and upbringing is Catherine, Guy's mistress. "Ma mère à moi croyait au ciel et à tout ce qui s'ensuit, justement parce que la vie est souvent trop salope, il faut bien qu'il y ait autre chose, quelque part" (238). When she admits that she too is a believer but still does not go to church, he reproaches her for not being logical. Being logical and consistent is, after all, part of Trovern's view of an orderly universe: "Trovern soupçonnait son patron Merlin de croire en Dieu—et même, de pratiquer sa religion: ce qui lui paraissait logique: Si on croit en tout ça, autant aller jusqu'au bout. Mais 'tout ça' lui semblait parfaitement inaccessible" (238). As this passage seems to indicate, Guy, the "hero" of the novel if there is one here, has not been touched by grace and has no knowledge of the supernatural.

Ironically, his obsession with a purely human and earthbound sense of order is expressed through the image of the gardens at Versailles. Upon one of his visits to Leroy-Bellègue's home early in the novel, Guy notices a seventeenth-century engraving on a wall. It pictures Louis XIV leading a group of courtiers through the harmoniously orchestrated gardens of Versailles. Trovern is so struck by the vision of order communicated by the engraving that he goes out and purchases an expensive photo album of Versailles—a place that as yet he has never visited—in order to contemplate the "perspective absolument parfaite des jardins, rythmés par les jets d'eau, les grands vases de marbre et le peuple des statues" (184). Finally, at the very end of the novel he decides that he will spend a day at Versailles: "il se baignerait dans le rêve beaucoup plus que dans la foule, seul, porté par un vent d'histoire et par l'ordre qu'il aimait" (288). Versailles, of course, is not only a symbol of order but also of a hierarchy of values. It also reflects a society, now vanished, that had a clearer sense of order than does the one in which Guy Trovern finds himself and that also proclaimed, loudly and officially at the top of the pyramid of state, a belief in God. This image of order, taken out of context by Trovern, represents Saint Pierre's attempt to inform his reader in an indirect way that Trovern is missing something in life, that he does not see the whole picture. The image of Versailles, like Dr. Erikson's meditations on evil as incarnated by killer cancer cells, is a means of depicting the central character's opportunities to experience grace, while at the same time making it clear that for the time being the gift of seeing and understanding more deeply and profoundly is being withheld.

The cinematic, rapidly moving quality of Saint Pierre's prose struck Paul Guth, who for years had been an avid reader of Saint Pierre's work. Recounting the author's typically vivid opening scene, Guth wrote: "Il filme l'arrivée de la police judiciaire avec la précision infaillible d'un documentaire." Noting correctly that *Le Double Crime* is both a mystery story and an attack on judicial laxism (as well as a defense of the police), Guth did not hesitate to call the novel "un des plus beaux romans policiers que l'on ait écrit depuis Simenon."[11] Yves-Alain Favre had the same kind of positive reaction. He wrote:

> Michel de Saint Pierre sait tenir son lecteur en haleine . . . l'intrigue ne faiblit jamais; ses rebondissements captivent l'attention. Néanmoins, le roman policier ne se donne pas pour but essentiel de nous distraire; il permet à l'auteur de nous présenter le monde de la police judiciaire et de nous montrer le drame qu'elle vit actuellement. Ce plaidoyer pour la police se double d'un requisitoire implacable; le laxisme de certains juges se voit condamné sans appel.[12]

Finally, Anne Muratori-Philip, also sensitive to the fast-moving, cinematic quality of the novel, wrote: "A travers cette gigantesque chasse aux assassins et cet hommage aux hommes de la criminelle, Michel de Saint Pierre a tenu le pari de préserver la qualité du suspense tout en sacrifiant à son éthique de peintre de notre société."[13] Constantly striving to develop new forms and adapt them to ever-new material, Saint Pierre, as he approached his seventieth birthday, continued to prove his mastery of his art.

9. The Last Novels

S<small>AINT</small> P<small>IERRE</small> <small>ORIGINALLY PLANNED</small> *LES CAVALIERS DU VELD*[1] <small>AS A</small>
two-volume work. Only the first volume was published during his lifetime.
It covers fifty years, from the arrival of a shipload of French Huguenots, all
refugees from the France of Louis XIV, to the establishment of their children and grandchildren as prosperous farmers far inland. The second
volume was to trace the history of these same people into modern times, but
Saint Pierre was not able to advance very far on this project before his
death. Thus, *Les Cavaliers du Veld* is a one-volume novel and will be
treated as such.

One cannot help being struck by the structural resemblance between
this novel and *Je reviendrai*. As in the earlier novel, Saint Pierre is more
interested in history and ideology than in writing a work of fiction.
Whereas *Je reviendrai* purports to justify and glorify Zionism, *Les Cavaliers
du Veld* sings the praises of the original white settlers in South Africa and
chronicles their advance inland at the expense of the native Hottentots.
Saint Pierre's formula is very much the same here as it had been in *Je
reviendrai* in so far as characters are developed only to the extent necessary
to tell the story of a whole people, the *bœrs*, or farmers, who are the
ancestors of the present ruling white minority in South Africa.

While these French settlers, originally selected by their Dutch spon-
sors because of their skills as tradesmen and artisans, are gradually merging
with the German and Dutch settlers who have preceded them (and, in so
doing, forming a new race that will eventually speak its own language,
Afrikaans), news comes to them periodically from Europe. Each of the
travelers who arrive in their midst reminds them of the incessant wars that

ravage the mother continent. Here, though, the three races have come together and live in peace for they have three common enemies that make working together a matter of survival. First, there is the Dutch administration which represents the political ambitions and financial interests of the mother country. This obstacle is overcome by gradual migration inland beyond the reach of the administration's military arm. Next there is the threat posed by the wild beasts that inhabit the Veld, the great South African prairie. Settling and taming the fertile land is made more difficult because of their presence. Finally, there are the Hottentots, the native bushmen of the region who resent having their land taken from them and who are willing to fight to keep it.

One of the principal characters of the novel is François Richemont, a minister of the Reformed Church, who is leading his flock to South Africa. He and his family, along with Alonse Joubert and his wife Barberine, constitute the nucleus around which the story, which is in fact not much more than a succession of sketches of places and situations, is told. On several occasions we find Richemont discussing the political situation at home in France where Louis XIV reigns as an absolute monarch. Richemont's remarks are amazingly ecumenical in tone and seem somewhat anachronistic to say the least. Not only does Richemont understand that the king would want to banish his protestants so as not to have any naysayers in the body politic, but he also concedes that the torture of protestants and the destruction of their homes and property is the work of his subordinates whom he cannot always control. Likewise, Joubert is presented as an insouciant, swashbuckling type of character whose actions are always brave and daring and who never gives a second thought to anything that he does. In a word, characterization in this novel is thin and it has a great deal of difficulty in supporting the ideological thesis that Saint Pierre is trying to defend here.

In the end, Saint Pierre's point is that the original white settlers in South Africa were driven out of Europe as political refugees. In this they are like the Zionists who migrated to Israel. That they found an untamed land and a hostile native population upon their arrival should come as no surprise. Here too, the analogy to Israel is obvious. What this novel is attempting to do is create political sympathy for a group of people who are usually scorned by the western media. The novel, however, is far from an ideal vehicle for achieving such a goal and this work is ample proof of that fact. Finally, although the various characters talk about religion a good deal in this work and in fact are religious refugees, the treatment of religion and religious questions never rises above a very low level of banality. In the final analysis, this novel as a work of literature is a dismal failure.

Michel de Saint Pierre died on June 19, 1987. Two days earlier he had submitted his last novel, *Le Milieu de l'été*,[2] to his publisher. As in *Les Ecrivains*, this novel takes us into a world that Saint Pierre knew well, perhaps better than anything else, the inbred universe of Paris publishing houses. At the same time, it is his last attempt to write a truly Catholic novel, a drama of conversion and salvation.

His heroine is Viviane Lancy-Villars, a director of public relations at a small publishing house in Paris. When we meet her in the opening scene of the novel she has come to visit Louis-René Marin, owner and publisher of the old and prestigious Lessac & Marin. She tells him that she wants to leave her present employer, Cassini, to come work for him as his director of public relations. She wants to do this because Lessac & Marin, benefiting from the prestige that comes with age, has nonetheless fallen a bit behind the times. In the course of their conversation she attacks a number of book series that Lessac & Marin publish and singles out the "collection catholique," directed by Quentin Louvier, for special criticism. To her, the publication of books that no longer sell well and for whom there is a very small audience does not make sense. Here, at the opening of the novel, the problem of the "écrivain catholique," his vocation and his audience, is put before the reader. Marin defends the publication of a small number of religious books: ". . . c'est une tradition de la maison, que la religion soit representée chez moi . . ." But he also acknowledges that the Catholic writer is an endangered species in France: "Hélas! Dieu ne fait plus recette! Je ne sais pas si je puis citer un seul auteur connu qui accepterait de se proclamer 'écrivain catholique' . . . je ne cherche pas à lutter contre ce courant, pas davantage à en examiner les causes profondes" (18-19). Although he is not interested in finding out why no one wants to be called a Catholic writer anymore and does not consider himself to be a religious person, he does suspect that there is some kind of existence after death. For this reason he is sympathetic to Louvier's belief that "Dieu nous suit à la piste" (19). This theme of God as a hunter of souls—and, in particular, that of Viviane—will be the main theme of the novel. Saint Pierre takes precautions, however, to present this pursuit in such a way that Viviane's change of heart about religious matters at the end of the novel can be explained either as the result of events that we know to have taken place in her life or as a result of the action of divine grace. The reader is left to decide.

There are three people who are close to Viviane: her husband, Hervé, her daughter, Carol, and her friend, Cécile. Although she also has a number of lovers, she does not share with these men anything more profound than physical pleasure. Viviane's husband, a professor of literature at one of the new campuses of the University of Paris, believes in the existence of God, although he does not practice any religion. He would have preferred to marry Viviane in a church ceremony twenty-two years earlier, but she would not go along with the idea. Carol, in her early twenties, is beginning to ask questions about the meaning of life, but has difficulty discussing the subject with her mother for whom the principal values in life are "l'amour de soi, le culte de l'être humain, la volupté de la chair et celle de pouvoir, l'orgueil de respirer une heure de plus . . ." (131). Cécile de Saint Maximin, Viviane's closest friend, is a childless widow who works as a reader for Cassini. As a practicing Catholic, she continually asks Viviane what she is looking for in life. After all, she is leaving a publisher who pays her well and treats her with great respect, she has a number of lovers and thinks nothing of deceiving her faithful husband, and her relationship with her daughter is strained because of a lack of interest on her part. Viviane is not sure how to answer such a question except to say that she does what pleases her and that sometimes people get hurt in the process. "Méfie-toi de moi," she tells her friend, "j'abîme souvent ce que je touche. Et je ne comprends pas toujours pourquoi" (52).

As Viviane assumes her new functions at Lessac & Marin, her private life suddenly becomes more complicated when her husband learns of her current affair with an aging writer and threatens to kill him if he continues to see Viviane. Meanwhile, the inevitable clash between Viviane and Quentin Louvier, the traditionalist Catholic editor of Lessac & Marin's "collection catholique," begins when Viviane tells him that he is a slave to his religion: "Je déteste les programmes et n'importe quelle espèce de servitude—y compris les servitudes religieuses," she says (66). When he claims that he is as free intellectually as anyone else, she scoffs at him. At the first full meeting of the editorial board, Marin ends up by accepting a scabrous book, *Le Sourire du diable*, proposed by Viviane, while turning down Louvier's suggestion of a traditional work of piety entitled *Pourquoi je crois en Dieu*. She has taken over at Lessac & Marin and crushed all resistance.

Viviane seems to be at the height of her powers when word comes that her husband has died in an automobile accident after having quarreled with her about one of her lovers. Knowing the circumstances of his death, however, she clearly understands that he has committed suicide. Among the many letters of condolence that she receives is one from Louvier, her enemy, who tells her that "Dieu, ce chasseur, est sur vos traces" (82). A few months later *Le Sourire du diable* receives a prestigious literary prize, thus reinforcing her power and making it clear that Louvier will have to go as literary director at Lessac & Marin. Since Marin no longer listens to him or takes his advice, he feels superfluous. In leaving, he becomes another one of Viviane's victims. Finally, Carol keeps on trying to find out what her parents had been arguing about the morning of her father's death. She suspects that something was wrong in her parent's relationship and that her mother was at fault. "Non, Maman," she tells her, "J'ai fini par le comprendre. Tu n'as jamais aimé que toi-même" (114).

This rejection by her daughter gradually begins to sow doubts in her mind about her way of living and she begins to wonder if perhaps there might be a possibility that God exists. When, a few weeks later, Carol falls ill from meningitis and comes close to dying, Viviane undergoes a crisis. Throughout this experience, Quentin Louvier, whom Viviane had earlier unsuccessfully tried to seduce as a further humiliation to him, remains in touch with her. Finally, at the end of the novel, when it has become apparent that Carol will live, Viviane and Louvier discuss once again the meaning of life and the role of faith. When she tells him how Carol, who has now decided to become a Christian, had been influenced by Claudel's dramatic experience of divine grace, Louvier listens patiently. Quoting Claudel, she tells him: "En un instant, mon cœur fut touché et je crus. Je crus d'une telle force d'adhésion, d'un tel soulèvement de tout mon être . . . " (188). This recounting of the experience of conversion makes the reader wonder if Viviane is experiencing the same type of infusion of grace as the one described by Claudel. When she had found out that this conversion had taken place at Notre Dame Cathedral, she decided to go there herself. "J'ai voulu revoir Notre Dame," she tells him, "que j'ai trouvé magnifique et vide—et j'y éprouvai cependent une joie confuse, inexplicable. Comprenez-moi bien, Quentin, je ne veux pas tricher avec moi-même. Je ne cherche pas Dieu, je cherche Carol." As she justifies her actions to Louvier, the reader can understand her motives. Carol is the most important person in her life and has come close to death. In addition, Viviane still has not been able to understand what role her new-found faith might have had in her recovery. Thus, as the novel ends, Viviane is asking herself questions about religious faith that she had never asked before. Is she then on the brink of conversion? Wisely, Saint Pierre steps back from answering this question and in fact the question itself is asked only indirectly.

In his last novel, Michel de Saint Pierre succeeded in devoting virtually the whole work to the question of Christian faith in the context of modern society. Although he sets the action in the publishing industry and in so doing uncovers for us the dark underside of this world (nepotism, the use of ghost writers, the politics of literary prizes, *inter alia*), the religious question is never very far from the reader's attention. In other words, even though we enter the world of publishing here in much the same way that we penetrate the computer industry in *Le Milliardaire* and the legal system in *L'Accusée*, it is still primarily a Catholic novel. The ultimate question of the saving and damning of Carol's soul is not answered directly, but the direction in which she is headed is hinted at. After all, the true Catholic novel should not be heavy-handed and seeks to treat this question indirectly, by allusion, and not by direct statement.

The most that we can venture to say is that Saint Pierre wants the reader to see that his heroine, in experiencing the earliest stages of conversion, is being pursued by God. Even though she tells herself that she had wanted to visit Notre Dame to relive her daughter's experience, and that she is seeking deeper contact with her daughter and not with God, Quentin Louvier has the last word when he says: "C'est la même chose" (188). What he means is that for the believer, God works through people and situations, not in a vacuum.

Saint Pierre ended his career with a fine piece of writing, for the book places directly before the reader the question of religious belief in a desacralized society. It also brings up the role of the Catholic writer in contemporary French literature. Several times in the course of the novel various characters cite the famous sentence that André Gide wrote to François Mauriac about the Catholic novel in the twenties, that "ce n'est pas avec de bons sentiments que l'on fait de la bonne littérature." Saint Pierre in his last work was aware of this challenge and clearly tried to write a novel that would be uplifting without being pietistic and that would raise important questions without loading the text with answers to those questions. In my view, he succeeded admirably in this final effort.

10. Conclusion

MICHEL DE SAINT PIERRE'S CAREER ILLUSTRATES QUITE CLEARLY that over the past forty years the tradition of the Catholic novel has remained an active force in French letters. This is not to say that Saint Pierre was a great novelist or even a writer of the first rank. On the contrary, his achievement as a novelist is on the whole somewhat more modest than this. At the same time, his truly important books, the most important of which is in my view *Les Nouveaux Prêtres,* still have not received the attention that they deserve.

The principal intent of the present study has been to demonstrate that Michel de Saint Pierre produced a body of work in his lifetime that is worthy of serious study. While there is no doubt that Saint Pierre saw himself as an "écrivain chrétien" and as such took it upon himself to speak from time to time for what he called the silent majority of French Catholics (as in the crisis regarding the proposed nationalization of France's Catholic schools in the early eighties or in his founding the Association Credo to bring together traditionalists concerned about liturgical changes wrought by Vatican II), he still felt that he was primarily a fiction writer and only secondarily a literary personality and pamphleteer. But this did not mean that he felt constrained to compose consciously a "roman catholique" every time that he wrote a novel. Preferring instead since about 1970 to call himself an "écrivain témoin de son temps" rather than a "romancier catholique" or "romancier chrétien," which he had used earlier in his career, he seemed to be attempting to establish the principle that although he was first and foremost a "Christian writer," all of his fictional works did not have to be primarily "Catholic." In addition, I hope to have shown that in those novels where the term "roman catholique" clearly applies, some novels are more "Catholic" than others while, from another point of view, some are more successful than others as fiction.

Most of Saint Pierre's novels, including works published almost forty years ago like *La Mer à boire*, are still in print and are re-edited regularly by various mass paperback publishers like Livre de Poche and Folio. To my mind, this wide reading audience is a significant barometer of Saint Pierre's talent as a novelist. As long as his work is discovered and read by new generations of readers, it will continue to live.

The day after Saint Pierre's death *Le Figaro* published a long article by Jacques de Ricaumont about his life and work. In a sidebar, it included a list of no less than twenty-four of Saint Pierre's books that were still in print. This is a formidable number of books to have on the market at any one time, and it is eloquent proof of Saint Pierre's wide audience. Like the eulogies in other Paris dailies, the one by Ricaumont stressed Saint Pierre's penchant for supporting unpopular causes, like his sympathy for Mgr. Lefebvre and his outspoken support of Israel and South Africa. As was so often the case during Saint Pierre's lifetime, the intent was to praise Saint Pierre for his political courage, but the result was to detract from the man's achievement as a novelist. For Ricaumont, *Les Aristocrates* and *Les Nouveaux Aristocrates* rank very high on the list of Saint Pierre's literary achievements, but to him the masterpiece is *La Passion de l'abbé Delance*. He writes:

> Mais à mes yeux, son chef-d'œuvre reste *La Passion de l'abbé Delance*, où il a montré un certain prêtre, proche par certains côtés du curé de campagne de Bernanos, victime des pires traitements de la part de ses supérieurs, contraint d'abandonner sa paroisse "comme un voleur", mais comblé de consolations par le Seigneur qui lui accorde, selon ses vœux, l'échange de ses yeux contre la vue d'une jeune aveugle, puis lui octroie le privilège des stigmates.[1]

I have had occasion to discuss above the relative merits of this novel in comparison with Saint Pierre's other fictional efforts, some of which I have ranked more highly. My point, however, and the reason why I quote Ricaumont here, is to underline my conviction that the time has come to begin the process of evaluating Saint Pierre's massive fictional output. The present study is intended as a first tentative contribution to that process.

Chief among Saint Pierre's novels as a candidate for reappraisal is *Les Nouveaux Prêtres*. It is clearly the work that is the most generally associated with his name. However, like so many books that arouse public controversy, even litigation, its value as a literary work has been forgotten. Dealing with one of the major issues of our age, the proper role of the sacred (as embodied in the priest) in an increasingly skeptical and secular age, it has much to tell us. In fact, the "new" priests of the title, the worldly ones who seemed in some eyes to be such fictional caricatures a generation ago, now clearly emerge in our era of "liberation theology" as true apostles. The prophetic element in the novel is also now more apparent, as is the eternal struggle of man to give new outward forms to his inner beliefs and convictions.

Beyond *Les Nouveaux Prêtres*, *Les Murmures de Satan* ranks as Saint Pierre's other major Catholic novel. It is the one in which the psychological analysis of the major character is the most profound and it takes us to the heart of Jean Dewinter's search for sanctity. Like *Les Nouveaux Prêtres*, this is also a prophetic work, especially when we recall that it was written several years before Vatican II. As Dewinter seeks perfection through the cultivation of what he sees as a more specifically Christian style of life—a communal existence that combines his family life with that of others—the novel takes us beyond the threshold of that nebulous area of life in which self-knowledge and self-deception, grace and the temptation to despair, intermingle.

In conclusion, I hope in the coming years to devote book-length studies to the work of other writers of Michel de Saint Pierre's generation. In so doing, I hope to show other aspects of the health and diversity of the Catholic novel in France over the past forty years.

11. Notes

Chapter One

[1]See our essay "Catholic Writers in France: The Generation of 1915," *Renascence*, (XXXVI, Nos. 1-2, 1983-84), pp. 3-16. The whole double issue is devoted to writers of this generation, including an article on each of the writers mentioned here.

[2]Much has been written on the role of intellectuals in French society in recent years. See, for instance: Jean-François Revel, *La Cabale des dévots* (Paris: Julliard, 1962), Régis Debray, *Le Pouvoir intellectuel en France* (Paris: Ramsey, 1979), Hervé Hamon and Patrick Rotman, *Les Intellocrates* (Paris: Ramsey, 1980), and Bernard-Henri Lévy, *L'Eloge des intellectuels* (Paris: Grasset, 1987).

[3]John Ardagh, *France in the 80's* (London: Penguin, 1982), p. 544.

[4]Ibid., p. 545.

[5]Ibid., p. 547.

[6]Among a number of interesting books on this major historical event, see: Henri Fesquet, *Le Journal du Concile* (Paris: Morel, 1966), translated by Bernard Murchland as *The Drama of Vatican II, June 1962 - December 1965* (New York: Random House: 1967); Xavier Rynne, *Letters from Vatican City* (New York: Farrar, Straus: 1963) and *The Fourth Session* (New York: Farrar, Straus and Giroux, 1966). Finally, the documents promulgated at the Council are gathered in Walter M. Abbott, S.J., *The Documents of Vatican II* (New York: America Press, 1966).

[7]Louis de Saint Pierre, *Rollon devant l'histoire, les origines* (Paris: Peyronnet, 1949). Louis de Saint Pierre offers a biographical overview of Marshall Soult's life in his extensive introduction to his edition of his ancestor's memoirs: Soult, Nicolas Jean de Dieu, *Mémoires du Maréchal Soult: Espagne et Portugal*, texte établi et présenté par Louis et Antoinette de Saint Pierre (Paris: Hachette, 1955).

[8]His pamphlet, *Plaidoyer pour l'amnistie* (Paris: Esprit Nouveau, 1963), led to a private interview with De Gaulle, but no prisoners were released as a result of it.

[9]*Lettre ouverte aux assassins de l'école libre* (Paris: Albin Michel, 1982) is a virulent pamphlet addressed to President Mitterand in which Saint Pierre attempts to rally resistance to the planned integration of France's Catholic schools into a common system envisioned as a "service public unifié et laïque."

[10]Saint Pierre wrote warmly of these six years of boarding school in Versailles: "Pendant six ans, je fus l'élève des pères Eudistes au collège Saint-Jean-de Béthune (Versailles). J'en ai gardé le souvenir de magnifiques années. Oh! je n'étais pas un modèle—loin de la! . . . Indépendant et querelleur, je devais cependant m'incliner devant la discipline exemplaire du collège et devant la culture de nos maîtres. . . . Entre la dixième et la dix-septième année, avoir vécu dans la proximité du Dieu de l'hostie, respiré son souffle, agi en pleine confiance avec lui, prié avec la simplicité de la parole quotidienne, adoré la Trinité sainte parmi ce bruit d'eau vive que fait une ferveur enfantine, voilà l'héritage de mon Ecole catholique." *Lettre ouverte*, pp. 209-10.

[11]J. C. Whitehouse, "Catholic Writing: Some Basic Notions, Some Criticisms, and a Tentative Reply, *French Studies*, LXXXIII (April 1978), pp. 241-49.

[12]John Cruickshank, "The Novel and Christian Belief" in *French Literature and Its Background*, VI (Oxford, Oxford U P, 1970), p. 185.

[13]See: J. Hillis Miller, "Religion and Literature," in *The Relations of Literary Study: Essays on Interdisciplinary Contributions*, ed. James Thorpe (New York: Modern Language Association, 1967), pp. 69-81.

[14]Maurice Bruézière, *Histoire descriptive de la littérature contemporaine* (Paris: Berger-Levrault, 1975) Vol I, p. 155.

[15]François Mauriac, *Œuvres romanesques et théâtrales complètes*, ed. Jacques Petit, (Paris: Gallimard, 1981), III, p. 1310.

[16]*Crossroads: Essays on the Catholic Novelists*, (York, SC: French Literature Publishing Co., 1982), p. vii. This useful volume gathers together earlier essays by Sonnenfeld on Bernanos, Böll, Flannery O'Connor, and Graham Greene.

[17](Paris: Lanore, 1931), p. 384.

[18]Ibid., pp. 321-22.

[19]Jean-Laurent Prévost, *Le Roman catholique a cent ans* (Paris: Arthème Fayard, 1958), p. 200. Prévost also wrote two other books on the Catholic novel: *Le Prêtre, ce héros de roman*, 2 vols., (Paris: Téqui, 1952, 1953) and *Satan et le romancier* (Paris: Téqui, 1954). Another study by the Jesuit André Blanchet, *Le Prêtre dans le roman d'aujourd'hui* (Paris: Desclée de Brouwer, 1954), covers some of the same ground. Concerned mainly with the image of the priest in Mauriac's novels, it argues that the postwar decline in vocations to the priesthood, possibly gave birth to an increased number of novels in which priests were heroes in the immediate postwar era. Reading the book today, we can see more clearly why Saint Pierre's *Les Nouveaux Prêtres* was such a startling departure from the traditional fictional presentation of priests.

[20]Gerard Mourgue, *Dieu dans la littérature d'aujourd'hui* (Paris: France-Empire, 1961), p. 153. Another important contribution to the subject from the same era is:

Gonzague Truc, *Histoire de la littérature catholique contemporaine* (Paris: Casterman, 1961). To Truc, who devotes no more than a paragraph to Saint Pierre, the latter is "un bon écrivain qui connaît son métier" (p. 347).

[21](Paris: Arthème Fayard, 1976), p. 11.

[22]René Rémond, *Les Catholiques français dans la France des années 30* (Paris: Armand Colin, 1960), p. 17.

[23]*L'Evidence et le mystère* (Paris: Le Centurion, 1978). See also: Lucien Guissard, *Littérature et pensée chrétienne* (Paris: Casterman, 1969).

Chapter Two

[1]Published in 1948 by Calmann-Levy. The title is taken from a line that Saint Pierre attributes to Apollinaire: "Tu es las de ce monde ancien."

[2]André Bourin, "Instantanés: Michel de Saint Pierre," *Les Nouvelles Littéraires*, 25 novembre 1948, p. 1.

[3]Jean Mauduit, "Michel de Saint Pierre: *Ce Monde ancien*," 10 décembre 1948, 4e année, pp. 116-17.

[4](Paris: Calmann-Lévy, 1951).

[5]Luc Estang, "Actualité littéraire: l'ennui et le malheur," *La Croix*, 4 novembre 1951, p. 6.

[6]Emile Henriot, "La Vie littéraire: le roman dur," *Le Monde*, 7 novembre 1951, p. 16.

[7]Paul Guth, "Deux authentiques romanciers: Roger Nimier et Michel de Saint Pierre," *La Voix du Nord*, 26 octobre 1951, p. 24.

Chapter Three

[1](Paris: La Table Ronde, 1954).

[2]Emile Henriot, "La Vie littéraire: *Les Aristocrates* de Michel de Saint Pierre," *Le Monde*, 27 octobre 1954, p. 12.

[3]This character, modeled on Saint Pierre's father, the family genealogist, turns out to be the father of Gilles de Lontrain of *Ce Monde ancien*. In these early works, Saint Pierre underwent the Balzacian temptation to bring back certain characters from novel to novel. Later he abandoned the idea.

[4]Henri de Montherlant, "Michel de Saint Pierre: J'en ai plein le dos," *Arts*, 11 decembre 1954, p. 1.

[5]Michel de Saint Pierre, "A propos des *Aristocrates*," *Le Parisien*, 3 octobre 1972, p. 19.

[6]Jean Lacouture, *Charles de Gaulle I, Le Rebelle 1890-1944*. (Paris: Seuil, 1984), p. 818.

[7]Op. cit., Henriot.

[8]Kleber Haedens, "Michel de Saint Pierre chez les aristocrates," *Paris Presse-L'Intransigeant*, 18 octobre 1954, p. 2.

[9]Yves Gandon, "L'Aristocrate Michel de Saint Pierre," *Les Arts*, 22-28 décembre 1954, p. 6.

[10]Pierre Ascain, "Une heure avec Michel de Saint Pierre, aristocrate et écrivain de race," *Eaux Vives*, décembre 1954, p. 155.

[11]Op. cit., Henriot.

[12](Paris: Calmann-Levy, 1957). The novel was later rewritten with Pierre de Calan as a three-act play with the same title. It made its debut on 21 September 1959 at the Théâtre des Mathurins - Marcel Herrand and had a brief run thereafter. The text of the play was later published as: *Les Ecrivains, pièce en trois actes*, (Paris: Grasset, 1959).

[13]Emile Henriot, "La Vie littéraire: *Les Ecrivains* de Michel de Saint Pierre," *Le Monde*, 5 juin 1957, p. 16.

[14]Pierre de Boisdeffre, "Le Métier d'écrivain," *Le Journal de Genève*, No. 150, 29-30 Juin 1957, p. 150.

Chapter Four

[1]Gabriel d'Aubarède, "Rencontre avec Michel de Saint Pierre," *Les Nouvelles Littéraires*, 7 mai 1959, p. 1.

[2]Jean Blanzat, "*Les Murmures de Satan* de Michel de Saint Pierre," *Le Figaro Littéraire*, 18 avril 1959, p. 3.

[3]Henriette Charasson, "*Les Murmures de Satan* de Michel de Saint Pierre," *La Dépêche Tunisienne*, 16 mai 1959, p. 6.

[4]Lucien Guissard, "Michel de Saint Pierre: *Les Murmures de Satan*," *La Croix*, 30 mars 1959, p. 5.

[5]Pierre Grenaud, "*Les Murmures de Satan* sur les champs de bataille de la vie quotidienne," *Carrefour*, 1 avril 1959, p. 16.

[6]André Billy, "Un échec de la sainteté dans le laïcat," *Le Figaro*, 22 avril 1959, p. 4.

[7]Paul Guth, "*Les Murmures de Satan* par Michel de Saint Pierre," *La Voix du Nord*, 14 avril 1959, p. 14.

[8] Louis Chaigne, "*Les Nouveaux Aristocrates* de Michel de Saint Pierre," *L'Echo de l'Ouest*, 7 janvier 1961, p. 4.

[9]Emile Henriot, "La Vie littéraire: *Les Nouveaux Aristocrates* de Michel de Saint Pierre" *Le Monde*, 7 décembre 1960, p. 6.

[10]Lucien Guissard, "Michel de Saint Pierre: *Les Nouveaux Aristocrates*," *La Croix*, 5 décembre 1960 p. 4.

[11]Jean Nicollier, "Michel de Saint Pierre: *Les Nouveaux Aristocrates*," *La Gazette de Lausanne*, 18 décembre 1960, p. 17.

Chapter Five

[1](Paris: La Table Ronde, 1964).

[2]René-Marill Albérès, "La Vie littéraire: *Les Nouveaux Prêtres* de Michel de Saint Pierre," *Les Nouvelles Littéraires*, 14 novembre 1964, p. 1. The novel was brought out in the fall in the hope that it would compete successfully for a literary prize.

[3]Ibid.

[4]Georges Michonneau, "Au nom de mes confrères, j'accuse Michel de Saint Pierre," *Témoignage Chrétien*, 22 octobre 1964, p. 15.

[5]Anon., "Michel de Saint Pierre poursuit *Témoignage Chrétien*," *Paris Presse*, 31 octobre 1964, p. 6.

[6]Georges Michonneau, "A propos des *Nouveaux Prêtres*," *Témoignage Chrétien*, 8 mars 1965, p. 3.

[7]Gilbert Cesbron, "Les Enfants gâtés de l'Eglise," *Le Figaro*, 1 décembre 1964, pp. 1, 24.

[8]Michel de Saint Pierre, "Les Enfants gâtés de l'Eglise," *Le Figaro*, 8 décembre 1964, pp. 1, 4.

[9]Pierre Henri Simon, "La Vie littéraire: *Les Nouveaux Prêtres* de Michel de Saint Pierre" *Le Monde*, 7 octobre 1964, p. 16.

[10]Michel de Saint Pierre, "Réponse au journal *Le Monde*," *Le Monde*, 4 mars 1965, p. 12.

[11]Hubert Beuve-Méry, "A propos d'un roman: abus de droit," *Le Monde*, 4 mars 1965, p. 12.

[12]Henri Tincq, "La Mort de Michel de Saint Pierre: la sainte colère d'un traditionnaliste," *Le Monde*, 21-22 juin 1987, p. 24.

[13]Gilbert Ganne, "La Dangereuse Aventure du clergé progressiste," *L'Aurore*, 15 septembre 1964, p. 12.

[14]Robert Kanters, ". . . et délivrez-nous des nouveaux prêtres," *Le Figaro*, 16 décembre 1964, p. 4.

Chapter Six

[1](Paris: Grasset, 1971).

[2]Georges Bernanos, *Combat pour la vérité*, 2 vols., ed. Jean Murray, O.P. (Paris: Plon, 1971). I, p. 17.

[3]Michel de Saint Pierre, "Je témoigne de mon temps," *Les Nouvelles Littéraires*. 30 décembre 1965, p. 1.

[4]Jean Montalbetti, "Un Pèlerin de son temps: entretien avec Michel de Saint Pierre," *Les Nouvelles Littéraires*, 6 octobre 1967, p. 4.

[5]Luc Estang, "Le Romancier et le financier: *Le Milliardaire* de Michel de Saint Pierre," *Le Figaro Littéraire*, 22 novembre 1970, p. 20.

[6]Gilbert Ganne, "Le Defi d'un milliardaire," *L'Aurore*, 13 octobre 1970, p. 13.

[7]P. Berthier, "*Le Milliardaire* de Michel de Saint Pierre," *Etudes*, juin 1970, p. 180.

[8](Paris: Grasset, 1972).

[9]Jacques Vier, "Michel de Saint Pierre: *L'Accusée*," *L'Homme Nouveau*, 2 avril 1972, p. 18.

[10]Christine Arnothy, "Michel de Saint Pierre: *L'Accusée*," *Le Parisien*, 4 juillet 1972, p. 6.

[11]P. Berthier, "*L'Accusée* de Michel de Saint Pierre, *Etudes*, août-septembre 1972, pp. 301-02.

Chapter Seven

[1](Paris: La Table Ronde, 1975).

[2]Jean-Louis Ezine, "Sur la sellette, Michel de Saint Pierre," *Les Nouvelles Littéraires*, 14 juillet 1975, p. 3.

[3]Anon. "Le Roman d'amour de Michel de Saint Pierre avec Israël," *France-Soir*, 11 juillet 1975, p. 8.

[4]Gilbert Ganne, "Israël inspire à Michel de Saint Pierre un roman d'anxiété et d'espoir," *L'Aurore*, 20 mai 1975, p. 10.

[5]Michel Fromentoux, "Michel de Saint Pierre: à la recherche des secrets de l'âme juive," *Aspects de la France*, 10 juillet 1975, p. 16.

[6]Pierre Fritsch, "Michel de Saint Pierre: un roman sur le judaïsme français," *Le Républicain Lorrain*, 15 juin 1975, p. 12.

[7]Op.cit., anon. *France-Soir*.

[8](Paris: La Table Ronde, 1978).

[9]Saint Pierre did not write a biography of Padre Pio, as he did of the curé of Ars: *La Vie prodigieuse du curé d'Ars* (Paris: La Bonne Presse, 1959). For further information on Padre Pio, see: Charles M. Carty, *Padre Pio the Stigmatist* (Rockford, IL: Tan Books, 1973) and John A. Schug, *Padre Pio: He Bore the Stigmata* (Huntington, IN: *Our Sunday Visitor,* 1976).

[10]Pierre de Boisdeffre, "Michel de Saint Pierre: *La Passion de l'abbé Delance,*" *La Revue des Deux Mondes*, octobre 1978, p. 660.

[11]Ibid., p. 669.

[12]Ibid., p. 670.

[13]Ibid., p. 671.

[14]Pierre de Boisdeffre, "Un Grand Roman de Michel de Saint Pierre: *La Passion de l'abbé Delance,*" *Le Figaro*, 29 avril 1978, p. 16.

[15]Robert Poulet, "Victoire d'un vaincu," *Rivarol*, 18 mai 1978, p. 11.

Chapter Eight

[1](Paris: Grasset, 1980).

[2]Alain de Massol de Rebetz, "Si je n'écris pas, je meurs: Un entretien avec Michel de Saint Pierre," *La Meuse-La Lanterne*, 21 mars 1972, p. 10.

[3]Pierre de Boisdeffre, "Michel de Saint Pierre: *Laurent*," *La Revue des Deux Mondes*, janvier 1980, p. 168.

[4](Paris: Grasset, 1982).

[5]Jules Barbey d'Aurévilly is often considered to be one of the first modern Catholic novelists. Although Calvet omits him from his *Renouveau catholique*, J. L. Prévost takes him as the founder of the modern Catholic novel in his *Le Roman catholique a cent ans,* and Gonzague Truc assigns him an important role in his *Histoire de la littérature catholique contemporaine.* Saint Pierre feels a triple allegiance to Barbey as a Catholic, a political conservative, and a Norman.

[6]Yves-Alain Favre, "Michel de Saint Pierre: *Docteur Erikson*," *La Revue Universelle*, mars 1982, p. 67.

[7]Pierre de Boisdeffre, "Michel de Saint Pierre: *Docteur Erikson*," *La Revue des Deux Mondes*, août 1982, p. 432.

[8]Jacques de Ricaumont, "Le Drame des chercheurs," *Le Figaro*, 19 fevrier 1982, p. 6.

[9]Robert Poulet, "Le Serment d'Esculape," *Rivarol*, 18 fevrier 1982, p. 11.

[10](Paris: Plon, 1984).

[11]Paul Guth, "Michel de Saint Pierre: plaidoyer vibrant en forme de roman policier, *Midi Libre*, 1 avril 1984, p. 9.

[12]Yves-Alain Favre, "Plaidoyer pour la police," *La Presse Française*, 4 mai 1984, p. 7.

[13]Anne Muratori-Philip, "Michel de Saint Pierre: une aventure exemplaire," *Le Figaro*, 1 mars 1984, p. 12.

Chapter Nine

[1](Paris: Albin Michel, 1986).

[2](Paris: Albin Michel, 1987).

Chapter Ten

[1]Jacques de Ricaumont, "Michel de Saint Pierre: Dieu était le soleil de sa vie," *Le Figaro*, 20 juin 87, p. 16.

12. Bibliography

Primary Sources

1. Novels

Ce Monde ancien. Calmann-Lévy, 1948.
La Mer à boire. Calmann-Lévy, 1951.
Les Aristocrates. La Table Ronde, 1954.
Les Ecrivains. Calmann-Lévy, 1957.
Les Murmures de Satan. Calmann-Lévy, 1959.
Les Nouveaux Aristocrates. Calmann-Lévy, 1960.
Les Nouveaux Prêtres. La Table Ronde, 1964.
Le Milliardaire. Grasset, 1970.
L'Accusée. Grasset, 1972.
Je reviendrai sur les ailes de l'aigle. La Table Ronde, 1975.
La Passion de l'abbé Delance. La Table Ronde, 1978.
Laurent. Grasset, 1980.
Docteur Erikson. Grasset, 1982.
Le Double Crime de l'impasse Salomon. Plon, 1984.
Les Cavaliers du Veld, Albin Michel, 1986.
Le Milieu de l'été, Albin Michel, 1987.

2. Short Fiction

Vagabondages. Aubanel, 1938.
Contes pour les sceptiques. Henri Lefebve, 1945.
Dieu vous garde des femmes. Denoël, 1955.

3. Essays

Montherlant, bourreau de soi-même. Gallimard, 1949.
La Nouvelle Race. La Table Ronde, 1961.
L'Ecole de la violence. La Table Ronde, 1962.
Plaidoyer pour l'amnistie. L'Esprit Nouveau, 1963.
Sainte Colère. La Table Ronde, 1965.
Ces Prêtres qui souffrent. La Table Ronde, 1966.
J'étais à Fatima. La Table Ronde, 1967.
La Jeunesse et l'amour. Plon, 1969.
Eglises en ruines, Eglise en péril. Plon, 1973.
Les Fumées de Satan (avec André Mignot). La Table Ronde, 1976.
Le Ver est dans le fruit (avec André Mignot). La Table Ronde, 1978.
Lettre ouverte aux assassins de l'école libre. Albin Michel, 1982.
Sous le soleil de Dieu. Plon, 1984.
Henri de Montherlant, lettres à Michel de Saint Pierre, Albin Michel, 1986.

4. Biography and History

Bernadette et Lourdes. La Table Ronde, 1952.
La Vie prodigieuse du curé d'Ars. Gallimard, 1959.
Le Drame des Romanov. 2 vols. Robert Laffont, 1967, 1969.
Monsieur de Charette, chevalier du Roi. La Table Ronde, 1977.

5. Travel Books

Trésors de la Turquie. Arthaud, 1959.
La Côte normande, 1966.

6. Poetry

La Source et la mer. La Table Ronde, 1986.

7. Theater

Les Ecrivains, comédie en 3 actes créee au théâtre des Mathurins (avec Pierre de Calan).
    Grasset, 1959.

English Translations

Bernadette and Lourdes. tr. Edward Fitzgerald. New York: Farrar Straus and Young, 1954.

The Aristocrats. tr. Geoffrey Sainsbury. New York: Dutton, 1956, (London: Hutchinson, 1956).

Men of Letters. tr. Peter Green. London: Hutchinson, 1959.

The New Aristocrats. tr. Anthony and Llewela Burgess. Boston: Houghton Mifflin, 1963, (London: Gollancz, 1962).

The Remarkable Curé of Ars: The Life and Achievement of St. John Marie Vianney. tr. M. Angeline Bouchard. Garden City, NY: Doubleday, 1963.

The New Priests. Saint Louis, MO: B. Herder, 1966.

Secondary Sources

Alexander, Calvert. *The Catholic Literary Revival.* Milwaukee: Bruce, 1935.

Bessède, Robert. *La Crise de la conscience catholique à la fin du XIXe siècle.* Paris: Klinksieck, 1975.

Bichelberger, Roger. "Le Combat avec Dieu dans la littérature de notre temps." *Christus,* #102 (1980), pp. 370-84.

Blanchet, André. *Le Littéraire et le spirituel.* 3 vols. Paris: Montaigne, 1959, 1960, 1961.

————. *Le Prêtre dans le roman d'aujourd'hui.* Paris: Desclée de Brouwer, 1955.

Brien, Dolores E. "The Catholic Revival Revisited," *Commonweal,* 21 Dec. 1979, pp. 714-16.

Bruézière, Maurice. *Histoire descriptive de la littérature contemporaine.* 2 vols. Paris: Berger-Levrault, 1975, 1976.

Calvet, Jean. *Le Renouveau catholique dans la littérature contemporaine.* Paris: Lanore, 1927.

Chaigne, Louis. *Vies et œuvres d'écrivains.* 4 vols. Paris: Lanore, 1934-54.

Cogny, Pierre. *Sept romanciers au-delà du roman.* Paris: Nizet, 1953.

Cruickshank, John, ed. *The Novelist as Philosopher.* London: Oxford U P, 1962.

————. "The Novel and Christian Belief," In *French Literature and Its Background, VI: The Twentieth Century.* Ed. John Cruickshank. London: Oxford U P, 1970, pp. 185-204.

Dansette, Adrien. *Destin du catholicisme français.* Paris: Flammarion, 1957.

————. *Histoire religieuse de la France contemporaine.* Paris: Flammarion, 1965.

Debray, Pierre. *Dossier des nouveaux prêtres.* Paris: La Table Ronde, 1965.

Dru, A. "Catholic Humanism," In *French Literature and Its Background, VI: The Twentieth Century.* Ed. John Cruickshank. London: Oxford U P, 1970, pp. 128-42.

Fowlie, Wallace. *Climate of Violence: The French Literary Tradition from Baudelaire to the Present.* London: Secker and Warburg, 1967.

———. *French Literature: Its History and Its Meaning.* Englewood Cliffs, NJ.: Prentice-Hall, 1973.

Fraser, E. *Le Renouveau religieux d'après le roman français de 1886 à 1914.* Paris: Belles Lettres, 1934.

Ganne, Gilbert. "Michel de Saint Pierre," In *Messieurs les best-sellers.* Paris: Perrin, 1966.

Garcin, Jérome. "Du divin dans le roman," *Les Nouvelles Littéraires.* 6 mars 1980, pp. 36-37.

Gardner, John. *On Moral Fiction.* New York: Basic Books, 1977.

Gilkey, Langdon. *Catholicism Confronts Modernity.* New York: Seabury, 1975.

Glicksberg, Charles I. *Literature and Religion.* Westport, CT.: Greenwood Press, 1960.

Griffiths, Richard. *The Reactionary Revolution: The Catholic Revival in French Literature 1870-1914.* New York: Ungar, 1965.

Guissard, Lucien. *Littérature et pensée chrétienne.* Paris: Casterman, 1969.

Gunn, Giles B., ed. *Literature and Religion.* New York: Harper and Row, 1971.

Hopper, Stanley R., ed. *Spiritual Problems in Contemporary Literature.* New York: Harper and Row, 1952.

Keeler, Mary Jerome (Sr.) *Catholic Literary France.* Washington, DC: Catholic U of America P, 1938.

Lebel, Maurice. *Etudes littéraires.* Montreal: Centre de Psychologie et de Pédagogie, 1964.

Majault, Joseph. *L'Evidence et le mystère.* Paris: Le Centurion, 1978.

Moss, Robert F. "Suffering, Sinful Catholics," *The Antioch Review,* XXXVI (1978), 170-81.

Mourgue, Gerard. "Michel de Saint Pierre," In *Dieu dans la littérature d'aujourd'hui.* Paris: France-Empire, 1961, pp. 153-69.

O'Brien, Conor Cruise. *Maria Cross: Imaginative Patterns in a Group of Catholic Writers.* London: Burns and Oates, 1963.

O'Brien, Justin. *The French Literary Horizon.* New Brunswick, NJ: Rutgers U P, 1967.

Paulhac, Jean. *Michel de Saint Pierre: témoin de son temps.* Paris: La Table Ronde, 1972.

Peyre, Henri. *Les Générations littéraires.* Paris: Boivin, 1948.

Picon, Gaëten. *Panorama de la nouvelle littérature française.* Paris: Gallimard, 1968.

Pierrard, Pierre. *Juifs et catholiques français.* Paris: Fayard, 1970.

Prévost, Jean-Laurent. *Le Prêtre, ce héros de roman.* 2 vols. Paris: Tequi, 1953.

———. *Le Roman catholique a cent ans.* Paris: Fayard, 1958.

———. *Satan et le romancier.* Paris: Tequi, 1954.

Rawley, James M. and Robert M. Moss. "The Pulp of the Matter: From Melodrama to Catholic Fiction." *Commonweal*, 27 October 1978, pp. 685-89.

Riordan, Francis Ellen (Sr.). *The Concept of Love in the French Catholic Literary Revival*. Washington, DC: The Catholic U of America P, 1952.

Robinson, Christopher. "Christian Convictions," In *French Literature in the Twentieth Century*. London: David & Charles, 1980.

Rousseau, Richard W. "Secular and Christian Images of Man." *Thought*, LXVII (1972): 165-200.

Rousseaux, André. *Littérature du XXe siècle*. 7 vols. Paris: Seuil, 1938-1961.

Sonnenfeld, Albert. *Crossroads: Essays on the Catholic Novelists*. York, SC: French Literature Publications, 1982.

Thérive, André. *Procès de littérature*. Paris: La Renaissance de Livre, 1970.

Truc, Gonzague. *Histoire de la littérature catholique contemporaine*. Paris: Casterman, 1961.

Whitehouse, J. C. "Catholic Writing: Some Basic Notions, Some Criticisms, and a Tentative Reply." *French Studies*, LXXIII (1978), 241-49.

13. Index